Day by Day

www.**penguin**.co.uk

www.transworldireland.ie

Day by Day

Sister Stan

I look at every human being from a more positive angle;
I try to look for their positive aspects. This attitude immediately creates
a feeling of affinity, a kind of connectedness.

HH The Dalai Lama

TRANSWORLD IRELAND

TRANSWORLD IRELAND PUBLISHERS
28 Lower Leeson Street, Dublin 2, Ireland
www.transworldireland.ie

Transworld Ireland is part of the Penguin Random House group of companies
whose addresses can be found at global.penguinrandomhouse.com

First published in Great Britain in 2013 by Transworld Ireland
an imprint of Transworld Publishers
Transworld Ireland paperback edition published 2016

A CIP catalogue record for this book
is available from the British Library.

ISBN
9781848272613

Typeset in 11/15pt Berkeley Old Style by Falcon Oast Graphic Art Ltd.
Printed and bound by Clays Ltd, Bungay, Suffolk.

Penguin Random House is committed to a sustainable
future for our business, our readers and our planet. This book
is made from Forest Stewardship Council® certified paper.

1 3 5 7 9 10 8 6 4 2

To the many, many people who have
inspired and supported me over the years.

Essays

'Stillness' Anna Fiona Keogh

'Kindness' Tony Bates

'Gratitude' Abbot Mark Patrick Hederman

'Listening' Síle Wall

'With Mirth and Laughter Let
   Old Wrinkles Come' Lelia Doolan

'Soul' Brother Richard Hendrick

'Friendship' John Quinn

'Courage and Daring' Lelia Doolan

'Belonging' Sister Stan

Introduction

This book is organized as a walk through the year but it does not have to be read sequentially. It is a book that can be dipped into and read as a series of meditations that allow you to move beyond thought and into a place within you where you can be still. Always present, always accessible, these short meditations will, I hope, lead you to access an inner silence and a deep stillness.

Our experiences in life are common to all of us and yet each experience has to be lived uniquely by each of us. This book is an invitation to appreciate all our experiences, an invitation to live in the present moment and to share the living with each other so that we can understand it before we lose it, enjoy it before we miss it.

Perhaps most books like this have been lived before they are written. I can make no claim to be living out the full implications of what is written in this book. But I have begun the journey and these thoughts and reflections are part of that journey. They have come to me through the words I have read and through people I have met and listened to, and who have taught me that life is for living, searching, seeking – even striving; all have been sources of inspiration.

Here you will meet writers, poets, visionaries from the past and the present – some I know, some I don't know; some are colleagues, friends or family who helped and enabled me to encounter everyday epiphanies. They have also helped me to find the sacred in the ordinary and the mystical in the mundane. Above all, they are people who have helped me to live in the moment and to realize that everything in my life is significant. Significant enough to be a continuous source of reflection, meditation, revelation or reconnection.

Reading books changes lives, so does writing them, and this book has helped me to change my life. The thoughts and reflections do not belong to me, they came to me, from many sources and through many people, and they come through me to you. I hope they will be inspirational to you too.

Within this book there are nine essays on nine different themes reflected in the book. With great generosity and alacrity, friends wrote the beautiful essays which embellish and enrich the book and enable it to help the reader to unlock hidden gifts within. I am really grateful to Tony Bates, Lelia

Doolan, Mark Patrick Hederman, Brother Richard Hendrick, Anna Fiona Keogh, John Quinn and Síle Wall for their enormous contribution to this book which I know you the readers will enjoy and appreciate.

I would also like to thank Brendan Kennelly, who generously gave me permission to use two of his poems, 'Begin' and 'This December Day', and Siobhan Parkinson who gave invaluable help and advice with the initial text. A very special thanks to my editor Brenda Kimber at Transworld for her assistance, guidance and help in bringing this book to completion. Also, a big thank you to Kathleen Curley Clarke, Johanne Farrelly and, again, to Síle Wall who typed different drafts of the book.

Finally I want to thank all those who have been an inspiration to me in my life and who are all in this book in one way or another.

Sister Stan

Begin

Brendan Kennelly

Begin again to the summoning birds
to the sight of light at the window,
begin to the roar of morning traffic
all along Pembroke Road.
Every beginning is a promise
born in light and dying in dark
determination and exaltation of springtime
flowering the way to work.
Begin to the pageant of queuing girls
the arrogant loneliness of swans in the canal
bridges linking the past and future
old friends passing though with us still.
Begin to the loneliness that cannot end
since it perhaps is what makes us begin,
begin to wonder at unknown faces

at crying birds in the sudden rain
at branches stark in the willing sunlight
at seagulls foraging for bread
at couples sharing a sunny secret
alone together while making good.
Though we live in a world that dreams of ending
that always seems about to give in
something that will not acknowledge conclusion
insists that we forever begin.

1

The heart stands at the centre of your being, where you are at one with yourself, at one with all others and at one with the true spirit of love that some of us call God.

When you see with the heart, you discover that there is no part of life that doesn't contain a surprise. No part is too simple or small, no part is too ordinary or extraordinary. Everything becomes full of potential, full of surprise.

> *The heart has its reasons which reason*
> *does not understand.*
>
> Blaise Pascal

2

We can't all live in close contact with the earth, but we can get to know our own space upon the earth. Spend time out of doors, celebrate the earth, reverence it, give thanks for it.

All are but parts of one stupendous whole,
whose body Nature is, and God the soul.

Alexander Pope

3

Driving to work, in a traffic jam, under stress, under time pressure, bored, worried, hassled. All those other cars out there are driven by people too, maybe also bored, worried, hassled. Try to look beyond the exterior, the façade, and send them blessings.

It's not what you look at that matters, it's what you see.

Henry David Thoreau

4

You cannot love anyone without experiencing the pain in yourself. When you truly experience and know your own pain, then you can reach out to lessen the intensity of another's pain.

Our greatest glory is not in never failing,
but in rising up every time we fail.

Ralph Waldo Emerson

5

Strive for a world where a passion for mercy and justice makes it possible to choose the common good, and do it in deep gratitude for those poor and powerless and homeless people who inspire your passion for the possible.

Everything is possible for him who believes.

Mark 9: 23

6

Every tiny detail in the living world is down to adaptability: the eye of an insect, the fin of a dolphin, the bone structure of a dog, the strategy of a reptile, the functions of the human brain. We live in a changing world – if you don't change you perish.

Blessed are the hearts that can bend;
they shall never be broken.

Albert Camus

7

Sometimes, you can get choked and stultified by your problems and by your own failings. Someone who loves you can show you that you are choking, and that is a great grace.

A friend is one who accepts both the chaff and grain.

Arabian proverb

8

Remember that until you increase your self-esteem by loving yourself in small ways, you cannot begin to change yourself in bigger ways. You must start by tackling all expectations, your own and other people's.

You are God's work of art.

Ephesians 2: 19–20

9

What are you willing to see with new eyes, to hear with new ears, to explore with a new heart?

We are called to be pioneers.
Pioneers who stand on the edge of great beginnings
of unseen futures.

Teilhard de Chardin

10

The Syrian hermit St Gerasimos once saw a lion hobbling with pain because of a bit of reed stuck in his paw. He brought the animal back to the monastery and took care of him, and there developed such a friendship between them that when the saint died, the lion laid itself down weeping on his grave and died too.

Friendship is always a sweet responsibility, never an opportunity.

Khalil Gibran

11

If you begin your day by worrying about what you have to do, you are probably taking on too much. Take things one by one and ask for help. If you accept your limitations, you will experience a new freedom and a new serenity.

One who pays heed to the wind will not sow,
And one who watches the clouds will not reap.

Ecclesiastes 11: 4

12

Everyone who has a job knows how work can eat into their personal time. In our culture, the workaholic is revered, and colleagues vie with each other to see who can work the longest hours, and who can look busiest. But even the busiest person needs to stop and take time out, if only for a moment. Moments of stillness and peace are always available. They are offered to everyone. It is all a matter of becoming aware and rethinking your values.

Real generosity towards the future lies in
giving all to the present.

Albert Camus

13

You have a hidden spiritual energy within you. If you tap into it, it can help you to move forward. You can learn to find this hidden energy by noticing, by paying attention and being mindful. Smell the roses, taste the coffee, feel your toes breathe, see the wind, hear the sirens.

If we could see the miracle of a single flower clearly, our whole life would change.

Buddha

14

The difficulties, tensions, pressure and negativity of the commuters' morning all dissipate when they glimpse the beauty of the morning sky.

Joy in looking and comprehending is nature's most beautiful gift.

Albert Einstein

15

Instead of wanting more, give thanks for the blessings you already have.

Let us try to recognize the precious nature of each day.

HH The Dalai Lama

16

HH The Dalai Lama tells us that compassion is the tool that can change the world. Jesus called us to be compassionate, as God is compassionate. You are called to reach out with compassion and conviction to people who are hurting, to places of pain and suffering. Through your compassion, you too can change the world.

Wisdom, compassion and courage are the three universally recognized moral qualities of men.

Confucius

17

There is a time for everything – a time for tolerance and a time for zero tolerance.

Without tolerance, there is no creativity, no love and no chance for change or growth. But tolerance does not mean countenancing injustice, or ignoring bullying and violence. Evil must always be faced and denounced.

Anger and intolerance are the twin enemies of correct understanding.

Mahatma Gandhi

18

Your inner beauty flows through your eyes, your smiles, your expressions, your gestures, your perceptions, your joy, your care and compassion.

Beauty is not in the face; beauty is a light in the heart.

Khalil Gibran

19

Every day you experience unresolved situations; unresolved questions well up within you. Do not be overwhelmed by these unresolved realities. Rather, use them as possibilities for new things. Stay with the questions, and insight is born.

Wisdom is often times nearer when we stoop
than when we soar.

William Wordsworth

20

Do not compare your talents and your abilities to somebody else's. Do not be caught up in a life of competition instead of a life of creativity, or you will lose not only your inspiration, but your courage and conviction too.

I have no special talents. I am only passionately curious.

Albert Einstein

21

You have only one moment to live and that
moment is now.

For in Him we live and move and have our being.

Acts 17: 28

22

The world is such a beautiful place. If you get
caught up with your own affairs, you can forget
that. Take the time to stop, look, observe. Beauty
surrounds you.

*All those who are unhappy in the world are so as
a result of their desire for their own happiness. All those
who are happy in the world are so as a result of their
desire for the happiness of others.*

Shantideva

23

In prayer you are dealing with what is first of all a matter of the heart. It's not a case of using, or straining the mind, but simply of uniting your heart to God.

Prayer is not thinking much but loving much.

St Teresa of Avila

24

Be comfortable in your own body and nourish it with healthy food and exercise. Nourish your mind with good literature, art and company. Nourish your spirit with silence, stillness and prayer.

We need silence to be able to touch souls.

Mother Teresa

25

Do not be concerned about things you cannot change. Concern yourself, rather, with what you can change. Do not take for granted the way things are now, or think that the way things have always been is the way they are supposed to be. Question everything.

Since my house burnt down,
I have a better view of the rising moon.

Japanese saying

26

Ancient proverb: An eagle can live to be seventy years old, but at forty, its pointed beak and claws curve inward and its wings become heavy with thick feathers. The eagle flies to a mountain and breaks its beak on the mountain wall. It must wait for a new beak to grow, and then it uses the new beak to pull out its old claws. When new claws grow, the eagle uses them to pull out its old feathers. Now the eagle is free of the weight of the past, it catches the wind and begins to live again.

None but ourselves can free our minds.

Bob Marley

You can marvel
at the sunrise and the sunset,
at the complexity of your own bodies,
at the beauty of nature,
at the comfort of friends.
These blessings are there for all of us.
Let us give thanks.

Gratitude is heaven itself.

William Blake

28

Sometimes as you look at a night sky, a single bright star appears, and in its brightness it transforms the night. Every star in the sky is changed by this new appearance. Christ is like that bright star, illuminating the whole world. You are also called to be a light in the world.

You have to find what sparks a light in you so that you in your way can illuminate the world.

Oprah Winfrey

29

If you recognize and do well what is needed today, the future will find you doing what is needed at that time.

He prays best who does not know that he is praying.

St Anthony of Padua

30

Joyful memories may seem faded, dimmed and weathered, but they are there, and you can revive them. One way to hold on to your most precious experiences is to keep a treasury, a book of memories of people, sayings, words, experiences, events – whatever brings joy to you at different times through your life. Then, when you look again at your treasury, it yields up its joys, as fresh as when you first experienced them.

A thing of beauty is a joy for ever:
Its loveliness increases; it will never
Pass into nothingness . . .

John Keats

31

The present moment is all you are sure of. The present moment is your only secure home. Living in the moment is living fully.

Do not dwell in the past, do not dream of the future, concentrate the mind on the present moment.

Buddha

32

Do not squander your unique and precious talents by comparing them with others'. What is yours is uniquely yours, and it is different. Accept that you are called to be yourself, to go the journey that nobody else can go, to create what only you are called to create.

To live is so startling; it leaves little time for anything else.

Emily Dickinson

33

Always wanting to be right can lead to closure of the mind and heart. If you are always right, you don't need other people. You can even think you know what God wants. But if you are to live a human life to your full potential, you cannot be right all the time. Keep an open mind and an open heart. You may not always be right, but you won't be wrong.

I delight to do Your will, O my God;
Your law is within my heart.

Psalm 40: 8

34

A sat-nav system is for when you really need to
go somewhere but when you are just taking a trip
for the adventure of it, enjoying not knowing
what you may find around the next bend, an
electronic system that directs your journey is
more a hindrance than a help. Getting lost is
part of the fun.

It's the same with life. It's the spirit in which
we make the journey that counts, not where
we arrive.

We are not human beings on a spiritual journey,
we are spiritual beings on a human journey.

Paulo Coelho

35

Each day is a gift to use as you choose. If you regard every day as a holiday – a day you enjoy, a day when you celebrate – you will be grateful for each day. And when you are grateful, you will be happy.

You will not reach love without immense gratitude in your heart.

Arnaud Desjardins

36

To speak of the human is to speak of the Divine and to speak of the Divine is to speak of the human. God is the depth dimension and a mystery. When you are authentically and fully in touch with yourself, you experience God.

It is necessary that this be the aim of our entire life.
In all of our thoughts and actions, we must be conscious
of the infinite.

Rabindranath Tagore

37

Imagine walking across a plank thirty feet above the ground. If you focus on your goal, the platform at the end of the plank, you'll make it. But if you take your eyes off the goal and look down, you'll fall.

If our times are difficult and perplexing, so are they challenging and filled with opportunities.

Robert Kennedy

38

Moments when you can bless and feel blessed are often those moments at which you are most alone, yet most alive to everyone and everything around you.

My body of a sudden blazed . . . I was blessed and could bless.

W. B. Yeats

If you try to tackle life's problems by yourself, you will quickly get exhausted or frustrated.

Learn instead to trust God. Let him carry the load. If you lower your burden and turn the problem over to God, the clouds will part and the sun will shine through.

> *What is more elevating and transporting*
> *than the generosity of heart which risks*
> *everything on God's word.*

John Henry Newman

40

When you have vision you do not see beyond the present but you recognize the depth of what is, and it replenishes your energy and the inner fire that urges you to live fully every moment that you are alive.

The charity of Christ urges us on.

2 Corinthians 5: 14
(Motto of the Religious Sisters of Charity)

41

If you try not to look ahead to tomorrow, but instead live today as well as you can, tomorrow will be happier anyway. A new day can bring new beginnings.

See how the lilies of the field grow. They do not labour or spin. So do not worry, saying, 'What shall we eat?' or 'What shall we drink?' or 'What shall we wear?' Do not worry about tomorrow, for tomorrow will worry about itself. Each day has enough trouble of its own.

Matthew 6: 25–34

42

To accept yourself is to accept your strengths and your weaknesses, your darkness and your light, your richness and your poverty, your beauty and your ugliness. That can be terrifying, and often, as Nelson Mandela reminds us, it is not your inadequacy that terrifies you, but your potential.

Do not refrain from speaking when it will do good. And do not hide your wisdom.

Ecclesiastes 4: 23

43

The first time I got reading glasses, a whole new world opened for me, a journey of seeing clearly and reading easily began. To see physically is to have possibilities and potential. But to see from within is to have insight and awareness of life's deepest meanings.

The meaning of life is to see.

Hui Neng

44

Instead of being dissatisfied with yourself, honour the robe that is given to you for your journey – a robe that is beautiful and a work of art.

Friend, hope for the Guest while you are alive.
Jump into experience while you are alive!
Think . . . and think . . . while you are alive.

Kabir

45

Rid yourself of anxiety and anger. Learn to walk with joy. Enjoy yourself and your own company.

One way to get the most out of life is to look upon it as an adventure.

William Feather

46

Pay attention to all that gets in the way of openness: your doubts, your fears, your needs. If you are willing to be fully present and to embrace life with openness, you will transform your uncertainties into new life, joy and wisdom.

Life is a succession of lessons which must be lived to be understood.

Ralph Waldo Emerson

Hope is promise.
Hope is possibility.
Hope is about what is not yet.
Hope is about what you do not see, but you trust
   is there.

> *Hope is the dream of a man awake.*
>
> French proverb

If your life overflows with gratitude, you send out
a message of love and a light that illuminates
everyone you meet. In that light, dreams become
possible, sorrows and losses are bearable.

> *Reach high, for stars lie hidden in your soul.*
> *Dream deep, for every dream precedes the goal.*
>
> Pamela Vaull Starr

49

It takes a lot of energy to carry bags of anger and resentment on your back. Forgive, and you will immediately feel lighter.

The weak can never forgive.
Forgiveness is the attribute of the strong.

Mahatma Gandhi

50

It is only if you choose to be attentive, to notice the small things around you, that you can learn to appreciate and relish life, fresh every day, and to open your heart to wonder.

Breathe. Let go. And remind yourself that this very
moment is the only one you know you have for sure.

Oprah Winfrey

Stillness

Anna Fiona Keogh

Stillness can seem like a vast empty space, and looking down into its expanse may make you dizzy. But when you discover stillness, taking even a little time each day to close your eyes and shut away the busyness of daily life, you will find that this great emptiness is already filled to the brim with what you cannot even imagine. Divine wisdom awaits you in stillness and silence.

> *After he had dismissed them, he went up to*
> *the mountainside by himself to pray. When evening*
> *came, he was there alone.*
>
> Matthew 14: 23

I wonder how long it would take Jesus to find stillness?

When Jesus went to the mountain, did he clamber all the way to the top so he could listen to the silence of nature and look down at the busy world below? Or did he go along the side to find a shady spot in the shadow of the mountain out of the burning sun to find rest from his work?

Did he gaze up at the heavens or spend time admiring the tiny flowers which grow in the most inhospitable of places? Did he pick his way along, trying to find the easiest route through the rocks and the undergrowth, stopping every so often to shake the stones out of his sandals? Did he allow himself to get lost in thought as he trudged along? Or did he begin his seeking of stillness the moment he left his friends and walked mindfully to the mountainside?

I was tremendously encouraged when I realized that even Jesus needed to take time to find stillness. I suppose I had always thought he just found 'it' instantly whenever he needed it . . . but it is likely that he too needed time to sink into stillness; to wait a little until the stillness began to permeate him and a sense of calm, priority and peace crept over him. He needed to turn his attention inwards to notice again the little pause between the inbreath and the outbreath; the momentary pause between each pulsation of his heart. He needed to go to a quiet space where he could be alone and where he could reconnect into the emptiness, with the Divine.

Stillness is elusive. It seems the most obvious thing

until we begin to ponder it, until we begin to look for it. Stillness is like a welcomed guest who we are hoping will arrive soon and will stay for at least a little while.

Stillness feels less like a stopping and more like a pausing in readiness. Stillness is not about freezing, or holding back, or holding in, or holding on. It is about letting go and releasing. It is about allowing ourselves to sit within the resonance of our living being.

It is the little pause between the inbreath and the out-breath. It is like when I balance on tiptoe; and for a brief moment I experience a sense of stability, calm and clarity.

Stillness is about resting. It is about resting from the hustle and bustle of the world about us, and the world within. This resting is a settling, like clay in water. Letting the soul catch up. Even the heart rests for nine hours a day.

Stillness is the sense of coming back to centre, of becoming realigned, and of connecting with what John O'Donohue calls the Great Belonging. It is a place where there is nothing, but where everything is possible.

Stillness is not necessarily about becoming physically still, though. I found stillness in a strange place when I discovered the physically active meditation practice of whirling. Perhaps you remember twirling and twirling and twirling about as a child, getting dizzy but experiencing a sense of freedom, elation and joy? I stumbled back into it through my dance practice as an adult. I found that if I allow myself to be lightheaded and accept that it is a dizzying experience; and if I let go of needing to feel like I am in control, I can turn and turn for a very long time, and more quickly than I expect, I begin to feel a sense of centredness. When I twirl, it does not matter that the world is spinning about me. I see it is spinning, but it does not matter. I do not need to grip the world with my mind: instead I have the sense that I am letting it go on spinning about me. I am aware of the present moment and I accept it. I feel my feet and my body as the axis between heaven and earth. It is at once an exhilarating and a peaceful place to be. It is the eye of the storm.

Somewhere along the journey of my explorations of meditation practices, I discovered that this practice of twirling or whirling is indeed a cultivated practice of Sufism, or Islamic mysticism. It is practised by the Sufi dervishes of the Mevlevi order founded in present-day Turkey by the followers of Jalal ad-Din Muhammad Balkhi-Rumi, a thirteenth-century Persian poet, Islamic jurist and theologian.

The word dervish (or darvish) comes from *dar* meaning 'door' and *vish*, which can be translated as 'to beg', 'to sit', or 'to meditate'. The image evoked is a doorway between two worlds[1]. A dervish is one who sits at this doorway. The dance is performed within the Sema, or worship ceremony. Semazens turn with the right hand open to the heavens and the left extended to the earth. Their turning represents a willingness to be in harmony with the wonderful and wondrous chaos of the world. Isn't this what stillness is?

Jesus gave us a prayer which I imagine he composed in his times of stillness, perhaps on the mountainside. I was taught these words at an early age and though I repeated them daily, I had little sense of their wisdom. As can happen sometimes, I discovered this wisdom when I found a translation of what has become known to us as 'The Our Father' in Jesus' original language, Aramaic (see over). It gave me a whole new sense of what Jesus wanted to teach us, and in it are words of wisdom which can guide us to stillness.

[1]Shakina Reinhertz (2001) *Women Called to the Path of Rumi: The Way of the Whirling Dervish*. Prescott, Arizona: Hohm Press.

The Prayer To Our Father

(from the original Aramaic)

Oh Thou, from whom the breath of life comes,
who fills all realms of sound, light and vibration.
May Your light be experienced in my utmost holiest.
Your Heavenly Domain approaches.
Let Your will come true – in the universe (all that vibrates)
just as on earth (that is material and dense).
Give us wisdom (understanding, assistance) for our daily need,
detach the fetters of faults that bind us,
as we let go the guilt of others.
Let us not be lost in superficial things (materialism, common
        temptations),
but let us be freed from that which keeps us from our true
        purpose.
From You comes the all-working will, the lively strength to act,
the song that beautifies all and renews itself from age to age.

51

Each moment is the place you arrive at from your most recent past and from which you step into the future.

We cross infinity with every step, and encounter the eternal with every second.

Rabindranath Tagore

52

When you are most alive, you are at your most spiritual, so take time to think about what it is that makes you really come alive. Ask yourself how best to cultivate the experiences that make you feel alive and in touch with the infinite.

May you live every day of your life.

Jonathan Swift

53

There is no such thing as a meaningless life – every moment is meaningful. If you are open to it, life will teach you how to be a person of wisdom, compassion and joy in our age.

Like the silkworm you have built a cocoon
around yourself. Who will save you?
Burst your own cocoon and come out as the
beautiful butterfly, as the free soul.

Swami Vivekananda

Surrender is not easy work. The ego drives of self-preservation and comfort make it hard to surrender to, or sign up for, life's hard lessons. Would you step forward if asked to volunteer for ill health or bereavement? Probably not, but you know from experience that you can handle these situations, you know people who are handling them.

If you surrender to difficult and awful events, you develop new ways of living and coping. You learn to hold what happens. You learn to deal with it. You learn to learn from it.

The art of living lies less in eliminating our troubles than growing with them.

Bernard Baruch

55

Life offers you choices. Freedom to choose is one of our greatest gifts. You can choose to believe that life is basically friendly; that joy can grow from the depth of pain; that life has meaning; that there are lessons to be learned from the worst situations; that growth is always possible.

Believe that life is worth living and your belief will help create the fact.

Henry James

56

You are called to risk moving out of security into a blessed vastness. And if you do take that risk, you will see yourself and your work from a new perspective, and you will not be overwhelmed.

Birds that live on a golden mountain
reflect the colour of the gold.

Tibetan proverb

57

Be generous, and you will benefit. You will become more willing to take risks. You will learn to set less store by possessions and more in people, and the boundaries between you and others will become more porous. You will feel part of a whole, and you will experience the joy of sharing.

He who gives to me, teaches me to give.

Danish proverb

58

Some dreams and visions come to you when you are sleeping or resting. At other times, you have to work on it and deliberately fit pieces of thought and ideas together and allow the design to come into focus.

Dreams are today's answers to tomorrow's questions.

Edgar Cayce

59

Learning to mind your own business is one of life's hardest lessons. Don't play the role of fixer; don't take responsibility for other people; rather be responsible to them, and for yourself.

The small truth has words which are clear;
The great truth has great silence.

Rabindranath Tagore

60

Anger needs to be expressed, because if you don't express it in a healthy way, it will build up and blurt out sideways and unhealthily in sarcasm or cynicism, or ferment into resentment.

Anger is a wind which blows out the lamp of the mind.

Robert Green Ingersoll

61

Busyness can keep you from receiving the joy of the moment, the joy of the day.

The living moment is everything.

Johann Wolfgang von Goethe

62

To be humble is not to run yourself down, but to appreciate other people's achievements and experiences. That's why it's so pleasant to be in the company of humble people: they treat others with respect and dignity.

What God requires of us is this:
to do what is just, to show constant love,
to live in humble fellowship with our God.

Micah 6: 8

63

Find a way to listen to the voice of the Divine. It doesn't require physical training or stamina; you don't have to travel to exotic places or holy sites – just teach yourself to be open and extend an invitation to the Divine presence to come alive in you, and then listen.

The world is charged with the grandeur of God.

Gerard Manley Hopkins

64

Life is a gift that comes wrapped in what you experience. If you accept this gift and open it willingly and purposefully, no matter what the wrapping looks like, you can discover unexpected treasures.

Each day provides its own gifts.

Marcus Aurelius

65

If you search out reasons to be grateful, you will find that you have an endless list.

What a wonderful day
The Lord has given us;
Let us be happy, let us celebrate . . .

Psalm 117: 24

66

If you want to be generous to others, you can make a huge effort and donate a large part of your savings, but you can also be generous in smaller ways: you can contribute some of your time to help someone, you can make small donations, you can pass on a book you have read, you can donate blood, you can offer to mind a neighbour's children when the parents are busy or under stress, you can give someone a lift. Whatever the gift, it is essential that, at the moment of giving, you give of yourself.

Give whatever you are doing and whoever you are with the gift of your attention.

Jim Rohn

67

The more you love, the more loving you become.

Our love is not to be just words of mere talk, but something real and active.

1 John 3: 18

68

We all radiate who we are. You can choose to radiate conflict and anger, or harmony and serenity.

When you are master of your body, word and mind, you shall rejoice in perfect serenity.

Shabkar

69

You are surrounded at all times by wonder, but
you may need to make a special effort to call forth
the wonderment that gets buried under the
demands of the day.

The world will never starve for wonders;
but only for the want of wonder.

G. K. Chesterton

70

As life changes, new demands require new
responses, new problems need new solutions. If
you find your responses are inadequate to the
situations you face, try to stand back and see new
possibilities that arise not from your head but
from your heart.

To see what is right and not to do it, is want of courage.

Confucius

71

Do you keep yourself constantly engaged with noise and activity so that you don't have to sit with the truth in your heart?

The authentic self is soul made visible.

Sarah Ban Breathnach

72

You know how it is: there's a driver behind you who keeps flashing his lights because you're not going fast enough for him, or there's a passenger on the train pushing to get off first, even though everyone else is getting off at the same stop. And you've also been on the other side: fuming and anxious while someone takes for ever ahead of you in the queue holding everyone up while she asks endless, pointless questions.

Such situations try your patience, and it's natural to be irritated. But if you can learn to practise patience, you'll get to understand something of the pressures that other people have in their lives too.

Patience is the companion of wisdom.

St Augustine of Hippo

73

Focus inwards for five minutes each day. Use the time to notice the thoughts that pass through your mind. Watch the process of your mind unfolding moment by moment, thought by thought, feeling by feeling. Try counting how many states of mind come and go within that short space of time. You'll be amazed!

All this hurrying will soon be over.
Only when we tarry do we touch the holy.

Rainer Maria Rilke

74

The blackbird would never know the delight of being carried on an air current if he did not spread his wings and leap forward into empty spaces. The swallows would never experience their long journeys over land and sea if they hadn't the courage to leave the nest and fly. The hawks that dive for food would starve if they were too timid to hunt and to soar.

Have wings that feared ever touched the sun?
I was born when all I once feared, I could love.

Rabia of Basra

75

The greater your awareness of each moment, the more you begin to let go of the stories that control your behaviour.

In the process of letting go you will lose many things
from the past, but you will find yourself.

Deepak Chopra

76

Stillness can seem like a vast empty space. But when you discover stillness, taking even a little time each day to close your eyes and to shut away the busyness of daily life, you will find that this great emptiness is already filled to the brim with what you cannot even imagine. Divine wisdom awaits you in stillness and silence.

After he had dismissed them, he went up to
the mountainside by himself to pray. When evening
came, he was there alone.

Matthew 14: 23

77

An easy ride can't teach you how to handle a dangerous bumpy road.

Smooth seas do not make skilful sailors.

African proverb

78

The supermarket cashier who opens a carton of eggs for a customer, to make sure none is broken; the motor mechanic who comes to your rescue after hours; the teacher who gives time to listen to students; the nurse who sits a bit longer to explain things to an anxious patient – these people are working beyond the requirements of their contracts. That is generosity at work.

When you practise gratefulness, there is a sense of respect towards others.

HH The Dalai Lama

79

Grateful awareness can open you to aliveness, whereas being on your guard, trying to maintain control, can close you down and drain the life out of you.

Let gratitude be the pillow on which you
say your nightly prayer.

Maya Angelou

80

Take responsibility for your anger and learn to be assertive rather than aggressive in expressing it. With practice, you can make anger your ally instead of your enemy.

Courage to the fearful, freedom to the enslaved, strength to
the weak, mutual affection to all sentient beings.

Shantideva

81

A good friend challenges you, but not too insistently or aggressively. A good friend's challenge is always tuned into where you are, knowing when to urge you to be true to the gifts you have received, and when to back off and leave you in peace. A good friend senses when to put a little pressure on you, and when pressure could dishearten or destroy you.

Be grateful for such a friend, if you have one. Try to be such a friend, if you can.

I would rather walk in the dark with a
friend, than alone in the light.

Helen Keller

82

A rainbow is a gift. It comes quite unexpectedly, apparently from nowhere – an invitation to stop and stare.

Pleasure is spread through the earth
In stray gifts to be claimed by whoever shall find.

William Wordsworth

83

The world waits each day for you who inhabit it. You have enormous potential and capacity. The world is yearning for you to be proactive, prophetic and persistent.

I want to be all that I am capable of becoming.

Katherine Mansfield

84

The best gift you can give your spirit is to nurture and care for your body. When your body is in healthy harmony, you can focus on your deeper needs. An uncared-for body, on the other hand, can drain all your attention and energy and leave little room or zest for the spiritual life.

To keep the body in good health is a duty . . . otherwise we shall not be able to keep our mind strong and clear.

Buddha

85

Generosity that is unwilling or cold or distracted is a contradiction. When you are truly generous you redefine your boundaries and reassess your understanding of what is yours, and a profound transformation takes place.

The best way to find yourself is in the service of others.

German proverb

Forgive yourself, forgive others, and you will live your life as a free human being.

Forgiveness is not an occasional act,
it is a constant attitude.

Martin Luther King Jr

87

Education does not happen only in the classroom. You can learn in almost any situation, at almost every moment of the day. Anyone you meet can be your teacher: a person who has lived through a situation you are going through can light the way for you; other people are often happy to share their experience with you, if you are willing to listen. The teacher, it is said, will appear when the student is ready.

Educating the mind without educating
the heart is no education at all.

Aristotle

88

You can't hurry life by taking tomorrow's breath today.

*Take rest; a field that has rested
gives a bountiful crop.*

Ovid

89

Sometimes the desire for intimacy cannot be satisfied at a human level. When there is a deep longing in your soul for closeness, an empty space that cannot be satisfied, when you feel like dry earth thirsting for the nourishment of water, this is the Creator calling you.

*I will instruct you and teach you in the way you should go;
I will counsel you and watch over you.*

Psalm 32: 8

90

Remembering is a kind of re-member-ing: putting things back together, gathering together personal stories and experiences, and claiming the past. You have to know and claim the past if you are to face where you are going to.

Things that were hard to bear are sweet to remember.

Seneca

Every time you trust, you put yourself on the line.
You know that in giving your trust you can be
cheated. If you confide in a friend, you can be
betrayed. If you have faith in a partner, you can be
abandoned. If you trust in the world, you can be
crushed.

But if you could be sure of everyone and
everything, trust would have no value. Trust will
cost you, but it's worth it.

None of us knows what might happen even
in the next minute, yet still we go forward.
Because we trust. Because we have faith.

Paulo Coelho

92

Now is all you have. Now is where God loves you, enlivens you, transforms you.

This is now, now is all there is
Don't wait for then
Strike the spirit, light the fire.

Rumi

93

Make a decision to see people as interesting and special, and you will find the world a fascinating place, full of possibilities and opportunities.

He who has no faith in others shall find no faith in them.

Lao-Tzu

94

A group of scientists had to carry out research in a faraway, inaccessible part of Africa. They came across a group of African carriers who were transporting their equipment by hand. Along the way, all the carriers inexplicably stopped at once. The scientists were astonished and then they became irritated and finally furious. Why did they not go on? They were wasting time. The carriers seemed to be waiting, but then all at once they started moving again. One of them explained to the scientists what had happened. 'Because we had been going so fast, we had left our souls behind; we stopped to wait for our souls.'

What is the soul? The soul is consciousness.
It shines as the light within the heart.

Brihadaranyaka Upanishad

95

The greatness of the Creator is everywhere in creation, including in you.

O God, how majestic is your name in all the earth!

Psalm 8: 1

Kindness

by Tony Bates

Mindfulness always sounds a lot easier than it is. At first glance, the invitation to pause, to breathe and to enjoy the present moment sounds positively blissful. But when we decide to give it a chance, we are seldom prepared for the resistance we encounter.

There is something about choosing to bring our awareness to our experience that can unsettle our psychological equilibrium. It's as if our minds have made a deal to leave us alone once we don't look too deeply. Bringing a here-and-now awareness to our inner life can mean facing feelings, memories and wounds that we would rather deny and disown.

So we may find ourselves rehearsing any number of reasons why today is often not quite the right time to meditate. While we may revel in talking about its psychological benefits, our actual practice may fall short of what we preach.

When we do 'take our seat' to meditate, anxiety can surface. In turn, our natural tendency towards distraction becomes even more pronounced. We may sit there fantasizing about anything and everything to avoid what is right before our eyes.

Thankfully we are not the first generation to discover mindfulness and we are not the first to struggle with resistance.

Many different traditions have identified kindness as the key quality of meditation that enables us to keep our seat. Many teachers of mindfulness have emphasized the need to infuse meditation with kindness, or as it is called in the Buddhist Theravada tradition, loving-kindness. They came to appreciate that kindness opens our practice and gives our inner lives room to breathe. Without kindness, they knew that awareness could be a blunt instrument with which we could beat ourselves.

So what is kindness? Intuitively we all recognize it when we see it. It's a fundamental part of our make-up that defines what is best about us. It is an energy that emanates straight from the heart. It is love, dressed in simple clothing. When we look at another with kindness, we see that person in a particular light. It may be true that they are behaving foolishly, but kindness sees through the self-centredness of human behaviour to the potential in all of us to grow and mature.

All of us are transformed when we're touched by kindness. Our hearts open and we sense we're in the presence of a person who doesn't judge, who accepts us for who we are and sees the good in us. In their company we are more likely to acknowledge the games we play, and to let go of inflated notions of ourselves.

To learn the true value of kindness, the poet Naomi Ney says that we first of all have to know sorrow in our lives. Her poem 'Kindness' says very clearly that having a full awareness of our own loneliness, our fragility and our mortality is what enables kindness to grow in us. It's what allows us to befriend someone when they feel most exposed and vulnerable; including ourselves.

Directing kindness towards oneself may feel odd. We are used to relying on our superego to remind us of our inadequacies and to keep us in check. To open ourselves to whatever we may be experiencing and hold it in awareness with kindness may feel counter-intuitive, even wrong.

In my own life, I know too well my own self-attacking mind. It never seems to sleep. I am familiar with its dreary motifs. Despite reasoning with its wild generalizations my negative thoughts return and sap my energy. As I take my seat for daily practice, I often find they have got there before me.

When I allow these thoughts free rein, my body tightens up, and old wounds are reopened. Their intention may be to help me grow but they do precisely the opposite. If they are allowed to take charge, they drive me down dark alleys of my past, where cruel thoughts, far from helping me to grow, immobilized me and kept me stuck in despair.

Kindness infuses our awareness with a positive energy that can counter our self-attacking criticisms. Kindness is the energy that makes practice possible, particularly when we feel low.

I had read about loving-kindness and while I found it interesting, I tended to see it as peripheral, a kind of optional extra to break up the monotonous routine of daily sitting. I find it fascinating how some things that come to matter so much in our lives can appear to have little or no relevance to us at all when we first encounter them.

I now begin each practice with some version of loving-kindness. I acknowledge that sitting takes courage and I nudge myself affectionately on to my cushion rather than gritting my teeth and forcing myself to do it. I express gratitude to my deeper self for getting me to practise every morning.

Kindness has made my practice more playful. I note with a smile the ways my negative thoughts come tumbling into my mind and I see them now for what they are: ancient demons that have passed their sell-by date; different versions of my ego trying to reject who I am; neurotic attempts to make me more acceptable to myself and to others. A painful waste of time.

This is not to say that I don't feel inadequate and broken sometimes when I now meditate. Of course I do, because at some level this is true, not just for me but for all of us. At some level we are all struggling.

It can be difficult to sit with what opens into our awareness when we meditate. At times when we feel low, we may find ourselves yearning for the time to pass so that we can make breakfast, drink a good cup of coffee and listen to the radio. What I have personally learned from sitting while under the weather is that it is precisely in those moments that I need to show up and be there for myself. To hold whatever is happening in awareness with kindness.

Kindness shines a light into dark corners of the mind and brings to the surface what needs to be healed in our lives. It sees all and it accepts all. Nothing is unacceptable, nothing is that surprising. And when we hold our pain in this way, we discover that it is fluid and that it is only our thoughts that turn pain into something solid and fixed.

Holding emotions and memories in kindness allows them to become unfrozen; their energy begins to flow. We see them for what they are, simply evidence of the ways in which life has touched us. With kindness, we eventually grasp why we behave in the way we do.

Kindness to ourselves and kindness to others softens our resistance to meditation. It helps us to drop beneath the noise level of our critical mind and touch the beauty of our lives, just the way they are.

96

Listening to others is a huge opportunity to learn. We all have unique experiences of life, of problems and solutions. If you listen to others, their experience can give you a rare chance to broaden your horizons. You can learn how it feels to be a member of a minority group; you can learn how to love yourself enough to combat hatred and destruction; you can learn how good can triumph over evil. Through listening, you can learn how to rise above adversity. And what is most important, by listening to others with respect and love, you can learn to truly value other people who are very different from you.

*The most precious gift we can offer
anyone is our attention.*

Thich Nhat Hahn

97

If you have the wisdom to be grateful you will walk unafraid into the unknown future, knowing that you are blessed and loved.

*Every step is an important advance
towards deep satisfaction and fulfilment.
The spiritual journey is like travelling from
valley to valley: crossing each mountain pass
reveals a more magnificent landscape
than the one before.*

Matthieu Ricard

98

You are constantly living on the edge of unknowing, called to make a leap of faith. Take it, and you will be glad.

*Belief consists in accepting the affirmations of the soul;
unbelief, in denying them.*

Ralph Waldo Emerson

99

The way you look at people transforms what you see. You are not like those video cameras in public places that register everything in an objective, anonymous way. In looking you give life or take life: your attention gives energy; your lack of attention takes it away.

The present moment is filled with joy and happiness.
If you are attentive, you will see it.

Thich Nhat Hanh

100

Hope enlivens faith and love.

Hope is faith holding out its hand in the dark.

George Isles

101

Learning to live in the present moment is a slow process, a daily struggle. But once you move into it and make it part of how you live, it brings great peace.

Forever – is composed of nows.

Emily Dickinson

102

If you put your feet into the middle of other people's lives, you'll get your toes trodden on, and you'll deserve it.

A false friend and a shadow attend
only when the sun shines.

Benjamin Franklin

103

Forgiveness begins with a willingness to free ourselves of negative emotions, and, perhaps, painful memories. If we are able to forgive we are often rewarded with peace of mind, and even love.

To forgive is to set a prisoner free,
and to discover the prisoner was you.

Anonymous

104

If you cling to past relationships and bitter memories, it may be that you are afraid to let go, to engage with the truth and so to move on into the future.

The only thing we have to fear is fear itself.

Franklin D. Roosevelt

I watched children coming into the Sanctuary one morning. They were greeted at the door by the teacher calling each one by her name: Katie, Irene, Ciara, Josie, Laura, etc. It made me wonder what happens to a child who enters a place where no one notices her – where she feels she doesn't count. To belong, to be accepted is so important to all of us if we are to thrive and flourish.

One of the deepest longings of the human soul is to be seen.

John O'Donohue

106

Patience is the skill of understanding and respecting your own rhythms and those of others.

Patience is the companion of wisdom.

St Augustine of Hippo

107

Did you know that a small tree can endure more than four hundred years beneath the closed forest canopy, and if the canopy is opened, it can sprout and grow rapidly?

Be not afraid of growing slowly;
be afraid only of standing still.

Chinese proverb

108

An unforgiving attitude brings ceaseless damage.
An unforgiving person is like a city whose traffic is
completely congested. The roads are blocked, cars
cannot move; they stand waiting, their engines
running, spewing out exhaust fumes, poisoning
the air. People are frustrated and immobilized; all
communication stops. No one enjoys life.

Forgiveness is the key to action and freedom.

Anonymous

109

When you have the courage to confront your deep secret fears, then you will be free.

> *For we have not come here to take prisoners*
> *Or to confine our wondrous spirits,*
> *But to experience ever and ever more deeply*
> *Our divine courage, freedom, and Light!*

Hafiz

110

This moment is all you have. The past is already lost, the future may be promising, but it is still a fairy tale. Only the present is, and it always is. There is no moment in which you are not in the present. You are eternally immersed in it.

> *If you are in the moment, you are in the infinite.*

Svami Prajnanpad

111

Giving thanks at close of day brings joy and peace for the night to come.

If the only prayer you say in your whole life is, 'thank you', that would suffice.

Meister Eckhart

112

The task of spiritual growth is to accept your human weaknesses and limitations and to love yourself in spite of your imperfections.

You, yourself, as much as anybody in the entire universe, deserves your love and affection.

Siddharta Gautama

113

A problem looked at another way may be a
solution. Mould growing unpromisingly in a pan
of water became penicillin when someone looked
at it creatively. It's easier to put up with life's
irritations if you can hold on to this idea. Rain
may seep into your shoes and make you groan,
but without it the crops would not grow and we'd
all die of starvation.

*When you change the way you look at things, the things you
look at change.*

Wayne Dyer

114

True generosity gives what the other person actually needs. It does not arise from a sense of guilt or indebtedness, or because the giver wants to create dependency or to show off. True generosity is a free gift; it generates freedom, and it is love at its best.

Generosity is giving more than you can, and pride is taking less than you need.

Khalil Gibran

115

Having a good laugh is like putting down a heavy load and sighing with relief at how light you feel.

I have seen what a laugh can do. It can transform almost unbearable tears into something bearable, even hopeful.

Bob Hope

116

It is always much better to be a beginner. You can make a fine impression as an expert, but as an expert you are less likely to take a risk because you have to defend yourself and your reputation. As a beginner, you have nothing to lose and are willing to learn; you can, and perhaps should, ask foolish questions in your search for knowledge.

In the mind of the beginner exists infinite possibilities, in the mind of the expert, only a few.

Zen saying

117

As surely as we modern westerners are destroying the earth, we could save it too, if we so chose. In today's polluted and damaged world, we need to be aware of our intimate connection with our environment, for if we destroy the earth, we destroy ourselves.

In nature, action and reaction are continuous. Everything is connected to everything else. No one part, nothing, is isolated. Everything is linked, and interdependent . . . Each question receives the correct answer.

Svami Prajnanpad

118

When you open yourself to the gift of the present moment, you learn to see with the heart instead of the mind.

The secret of health for both mind and body is not to mourn for the past, worry about the future, or anticipate troubles, but to live in the present moment wisely and earnestly.

Gautama Siddharta

119

Love is the gift of belonging. When you fall in love, your sense of belonging is powerful, your yes is spontaneous.

It is the sense of belonging that true love can give you, that makes you reach out to all, knowing that all belongs to all.

Let us not love with words or tongue, but with actions and in truth.

1 John 3: 18

120

In a world riven by conflict and war, you are called to be a peacemaker. This involves being at peace with yourself, so that you can be a peaceful presence to others. Peace comes from the heart and is nourished by the vision that all life is sacred and that every human on the earth is equal.

Jesus said, 'My peace I leave with you; my peace I give you.'

John 14: 27

121

Living in hope is living in a transforming presence.

Hope springs eternal in the human breast.

Alexander Pope

122

When you are fully connected to others, fully alive
to those around you, something of yourself can be
released to others, and you experience a special
awareness of the richness of your own gifts.

*Every time you smile at someone, it is an action of love,
a gift to that person, a beautiful thing.*

Mother Teresa

123

We live in a culture of achievement, which believes
that people get what they deserve. But this is not
true. Life is a gift that you did not earn; you are
called not to pay your way through life, but to live
in gratitude for the gifts you have received.

*Gratitude is the fairest blossom
which springs from the soul.*

Henry Ward Beecher

Have you ever felt that what seemed to be easy in the past is now making you anxious, stressed and irritable? Do you sometimes feel out of your depth and even frustrated at your inability to cope? Do you find that you haven't the time you used to have for family, friends and yourself, and no time at all just to do nothing or do something you really enjoy?

If you have reached this point, it is time to stop, to take stock, look at what is going on. You may not be able to do this by yourself. Maybe you can discuss it with someone you trust and who will understand – someone who can help you to work out where you are going and where you want to be.

Our ultimate freedom is the right and power to decide how anybody or anything outside ourselves will affect us.

Stephen Covey

125

It's easier to accept death when you think of it as part of life.

The fear of death follows from the fear of life. A man who lives fully is prepared to die at any time.

Mark Twain

For many years, I have been working with people who live in poverty and disadvantage, people who lack the basic necessities of life. I go into homes where there is no sign of comfort and I am amazed at the welcome I get and the generosity as people offer a cup of tea and whatever they have in the house. What sort of system allows me to have all I need and yet keeps such people in terrible poverty?

Look into your heart today and choose one action, one behaviour, that will change your heart and ultimately create a new world from the inside out.

The value of man resides in what he gives and not in what he is capable of receiving.

Albert Einstein

127

Love fosters kindness, love elicits respect, love clears the way for a positive attitude, and love inspires hope and confidence. Love brings joy, peace, harmony and beauty.

A loving heart is the beginning of all knowledge.

Thomas Carlyle

128

Living in the now challenges your need to fill every moment with action, planning and doing.

Do not let tomorrow use up too much of today.

Cherokee Indian proverb

129

Don't take your body for granted. You cannot expect it to keep working well no matter how you feed it, how little fresh air and how little sleep or exercise you give it.

The greatest wealth is health.

Virgil

130

As night falls and you look for peace and sleep, forgive what needs to be forgiven with all the love in your heart and soul, and let the day close as it began, with thanksgiving.

Thus all the lines converge,
complete one another, interlock.
All things are now but one.

Teilhard de Chardin, *Hymn of the Universe*

131

People often believe that poor people are poor because they are lazy or stupid or drink too much. Lots of rich people are lazy or stupid or drink too much, but nobody ever suggests that that is why they are rich.

If you judge people, you have no time to love them.

Mother Teresa

132

It is possible to so constrain yourself with worry and fear that even when God's own liberating joy comes to you, you don't open the door to it.

I have come that you may have life and live it to the full.

John 10: 10

133

When someone is bereaved, the only thing you can do is be there to listen when they need to talk, and be silent when silence is best. Recognize that the bereavement is theirs, not yours, and do not try to stop the pain or rush them through their grieving. They need love and patience. And they need time.

Unable are the loved to die.
For love is immortality.

Emily Dickinson

134

Your true self can only start to flourish when you let go of self-doubt.

It is not the mountain we conquer, but ourselves.

Sir Edmund Hillary

Some people make major contributions to the well-being of others: they donate large sums of money to hospitals or they perform big acts of heroism or they are skilled in saving other people's lives.

But a great opportunity to do good may never come your way, and in any case, the desire to perform great acts of goodness may have its roots in the ego and not in the heart. If you really want to serve others, there are small opportunities every day. Give a smile, a genuine compliment; offer to take someone to or from a hospital or medical appointment. There are always small kindnesses to be done for friends and strangers.

The light of love is like a morning star which lives in the heart of everyone.

Lao-Tzu

136

Peacemaking is not the same as passivity. It is based in love and truth and it is creative action that seeks justice for the whole human race.

Blessed are the peacemakers, for they will be called the children of God.

Matthew 5: 9

137

A daily practice of mindfulness can help to bring balance to your life, reminding you to pause, to listen to your heart, reminding you of your inner call to be an artist who continues the work of creation.

This Ariyan Eightfold Path, that is to say:
Right view, right aim, right speech, right action, right living,
right effort, right mindfulness, right contemplation.

Gautama Siddharta

138

The wisdom of experience can be gained no other
way than by simply living longer, growing older.

We do not receive wisdom,
we must discover it for ourselves,
after a journey through the wilderness
which no one else can make for us,
which no one can spare us,
for our wisdom is the point of view
from which we come at last to regard the world.

Marcel Proust

139

Humility is the best aid to learning that we have.
Humble students, assuming they know the least,
conduct more tests and research when given a
problem to solve. In this way, they become more
able than those who take short cuts because they
think they already have the answers.

Without humility there can be no humanity.

John Buchan

140

Here is a simple recipe for peace, available to everyone: do what you are doing. If you are doing what you are doing, then you are centred, you are there, one hundred per cent and so, in that moment, you are afraid of nothing and can need nothing. In that moment you find fullness.

Only those who have learned the power
of sincere and selfless contribution experience
life's deepest joy: true fulfilment.

Anthony Robbins

141

Memories can be a blessing, nourishing and strengthening you. This is what makes the amnesia of senile dementia so sad. The sufferer is always in the present, but it is a present without a history, without context. The sacred space is lost.

Every man's memory is his private literature.

Aldous Huxley

142

If you train yourself to look at the people around you with a more attentive eye, not only will you come to see their valuable qualities, but you yourself will grow too. You are, after all, made of your perceptions. What you see or presume to see, day after day, constitutes who you are and colours your whole life.

*It is not the answers that show us
the way, but the questions.*

Rainer Maria Rilke

Suppose you woke up tomorrow morning to find that ethnic group X has forgiven ethnic group Y, which in past centuries had oppressed it, violated its women, exploited its men, mistreated its children and plundered its possessions. What if nation A and nation B acknowledged each other's right to exist freely without fear and oppression, forgetting the wrongs of the past? Suppose even individuals had forgiven one another every injustice?

Then, for the first time, we could live fully, authentically and without malice, live without investing huge parts of ourselves in recrimination and accusation. Think of how all that energy could be used to create thousands of new projects that would be of benefit to us all!

> *Yes, this is what good is: to forgive evil.*
> *There is no other good.*

Antonio Porchia

Gratitude

Abbot Mark Patrick Hederman

If the only prayer you say in your life is, 'thank you',
that would suffice.

Meister Eckhart

Gratitude is ambiguous. Too many people in our world feel it is their due and your duty. Mr Pumblechook in *Great Expectations* keeps reminding the little boy, Pip: 'Be ever grateful to those who brought you up by hand,' and Pip wishes that they hadn't really bothered, or at least, hadn't been quite so heavy-handed. Parents often reproach their children about decisions in their lives of which they disapprove: 'After all I've done for you, this is my thanks!' As John Prentice famously replied in William Rose's *Guess Who's Coming to Dinner*: 'You listen to me. You say you don't want to tell me how to live my life. So what do you think you've been doing? You tell me what rights I've got or haven't got, and what I owe to you for what you've done for me. Let me tell you something. I owe you nothing! If you carried that bag a million miles, you did what you're supposed to do! Because you brought me into this world. And from that day you owed me everything you could ever do for me like I will owe my son if I ever have another. But you don't own me! You can't tell me when or where I'm out of line, or try to get me to live my life according to your rules. You don't even know what I am, Dad, you don't know who I am. You don't know how I feel, what I think. And if I tried to explain it the rest of your life you will never understand. You are thirty years older than I am. You and your whole lousy generation believe the way it was for you is the way it's got to be. And not until your whole generation has lain down and died will the dead weight be off our backs!'

'Gratitude is a disease of dogs,' Stalin suggested, pointing to another danger. Emerson puts it this way: 'We wish to be self-sustained. We do not quite forgive a giver. The hand that feeds us is in some danger of being bitten.' We cherish our independence and want to offload as many thank you letters as possible to the trash compactor.

Sometimes we over-compensate. Dermot Morgan's 1986 hit single about Barry McGuigan lampooned the internationally successful Irish boxer's fawning praise of his manager after every winning bout: *So I'm saying thank you, thank you, thank you very, very much Mr Eastwood. Thanks Mum, and Dad, and my brothers and sister. But the man I thank most is the man I call Mister. Mr Eastwood. Thank you very, very, very much Mr Eastwood. Thank you very, very, very much Mr Eastwood.* Morgan was pointing to an Irish trait: the Uriah Heep in us all. Tipping the cap, touching the forelock, while at the same time carrying a chip on each shoulder, for balance, and resenting every word that comes out of our mouth. Acting the lickspittle is often camouflage: the grovelling servile toady on the top is a back stabbing, splenetic, time bomb underneath.

As with every other human reality there can be too much of a good thank. We have to be careful about where and how much gratitude we plant. Kahlil Gibran has *The Prophet* say: 'And you receivers – and you are all receivers – assume no weight of gratitude, lest you lay a yoke upon yourself and upon those who give. Rather rise together with the giver on their gifts as on wings.'

All this suggests that gratitude is a virtue or an attitude which we can cultivate, adopt or curtail, as we see fit. In fact, gratitude should be the deepest awareness possible at the most fundamental level of our being.

Ontological rather than cosmetic gratitude is our goal. We may begin life trying to establish ourselves as an independent reality; but as we grow up we become aware of our innate dependency. We learn gratitude by learning about ourselves. Who are we? What are we? Gratitude is the way of being for those who understand that their life, their love, their every breath are pure grace, pure gift from God. We don't start out with that awareness, we have to come to that realization. We are not born grateful: we become it; or rather, it becomes us. Our natural reaction is to believe ourselves responsible for all that we are and do. It takes time and humility to realize that an unknown and hidden donor has sponsored our every move. Nor should this be an overweening discovery: should the mighty Amazon lament its humble origins in a mountain brook in the snowbound peaks of the Peruvian Andes? Or does the Great Barrier Reef blush for shame at the skeletons of tiny sea polyps that make it up? This is what we are, this is how we are made – and, more importantly, it is an intimation of the grace we are to become: a great barrier reef made up of billions of skeletons between time and eternity; a silver thread of water gathering itself into a mighty river before plunging into the Atlantic: images of our eternity in the love of infinity for ever.

Why should we not revel in gratitude for what we

have been given? We owe our thanks to God alone. 'It is right and just.' God is the giver of all gifts and everything we have and are, is gift. 'What shall I give back to the Lord, for all that has been given to me?' God himself came on earth to teach us how to give thanks gracefully. We call it 'the Eucharist', from the Greek word meaning 'thanksgiving'. It is a ritual, a ceremony which maintains the right balance between the human and the Divine, which makes us less awkward in the presence of the Almighty.

'She had opened dozens of presents from him. A turquoise bracelet, a tropical-fish tank, a vest beaded with Elvis Presley's visage, canary eyes and sequin lips. She opened the last box, glanced at him. Sitting with his hands dangling, watching her.

' "Wait a minute," she said and ran into the kitchen. He heard the refrigerator open. She came back with her hands behind her back.

' "I didn't have a chance to buy you anything," she said, then held both closed hands toward him. Uncurled her fingers. In each cupped palm a brown egg. He took them. They were cold. He thought it a tender, wonderful thing to do. She had given him something, the eggs, after all, only a symbol, but they had come from her hands as a gift. To him. It didn't matter that he'd bought them himself at the supermarket the day before. He imagined she understood him, that she had to love him to know that it was the outstretched hands, the giving, that mattered.'[1]

The Eucharist is the miraculous way in which Jesus Christ made gratitude acceptable. It is also the way He began the work of incorporating each one of us, and the world in which we live, into His body and blood. It takes time for us to agree and to accept this blood transfusion. We are inclined to resent the donor, and our system rejects the transfusion initially. But, once we understand that we are nothing more than a gift; when the truth sinks in that we have the option to become either gratitude or grief; then we are ready to make the choice between life and death. If we choose life, we can then throw everything away and allow ourselves to rise to another level of being where we enter the gratitude of God. We can make our own the last words of St Clare of Assisi: 'I thank you Lord for giving me my life'; or of Gerard Manley Hopkins on his deathbed: 'I am happy, so happy, I loved my life.' Everything in the end is gratitude because everything is grace.

[1] Annie Proulx, 'It's the Thought that Counts', from *The Shipping News*.

144

Each day new opportunities for love come your way. Take them.

Ultimately, love is everything.

M. Scott Peck

145

When you really live in hope, you do not deny darkness or negativity or pain, but neither do you give in or resign yourself to it. In hope you hold all the abuse and conflicts all around you, the wars, the misuse of power, the abuse and neglect of people, believing that the Divine power is greater than the tragedy you see around you.

All things are possible to him that believeth.

Mark 9: 23

Waiting can be painful. Waiting for somebody to come home, and worrying about their safety. Waiting for the result of an exam or for a diagnosis. Lying awake because of a sickness, a death, a disruption.

One way to cope with the pain of waiting is to turn it into a vigil. Vigilance is a spiritual discipline and a special kind of prayer.

Look at the stars! look, look up at the skies!
O look at all the fire-folk sitting in the air!
The bright boroughs, the circle-citadels there!

Gerard Manley Hopkins

147

If you pay attention, you can keep at bay the quarrelsome thoughts that continually try to invade and seduce your mind. In this way, attentiveness becomes a moral quality like love and justice.

We can always choose to perceive things differently.
You can focus on what's wrong in your life,
or you can focus on what's right.

Marianne Williamson

148

Respect for others, and especially for older people, is a sign of spiritual maturity.

Respect for ourselves guides our morals;
respect for others guides our manners.

Laurence Sterne

Distrust has harmful and disruptive effects on
people. Trust does the opposite: it aids and
nourishes you and it multiplies your possibilities.

> *Trust is the glue of life . . .*
> *It's the foundational principle*
> *that holds all relationships.*

Stephen Covey

150

It is impossible to know who you are unless you
recognize the journey you have been on, the
experiences you have had, and where and with
whom you belong.

> *We are shaped and fashioned by what we love.*

Johann Wolfgang von Goethe

Anger can be a pain in the neck – literally: it can lead to pain and tension in the neck and head. It can make your blood boil – or at least it can put your blood pressure up. And it's a natural reaction, if someone has broken a promise or stolen from you or injured or insulted you in some way, to feel tense and angry.

Your anger may be justified, and there is no point in ignoring it – because that way it will simply fester – or in giving way to it, exploding or imploding, lashing out at the person who has caused such pain. This can only lead to more conflict and more anger on both sides.

Try instead to make some space for your anger. Even if you just acknowledge that you are furious you'll start to feel better, and then you are already on your way to dealing with it.

Anger is often more hurtful than the injury that caused it.

American proverb

152

Human beings can thrive only in relationships, and that is impossible if you cannot read the emotions and intentions and needs of others. Empathy with the other is a prerequisite for communication, collaboration and social cohesion.

Love implies generosity, care, not to hurt another, not to make them feel guilty, to be generous, courteous, and behave in such a manner that your words and thoughts are born out of compassion.

Krishnamurti

153

Imagine a person who does not engage with you when you are talking to them. They look away or read the paper or answer you with something irrelevant to what you have been saying. Inattention has a disruptive and depressing aspect which saps your vitality and robs you of self-confidence, which is why it can arouse all your latent feelings of inferiority

Attention, on the other hand, is healing, energizing, life-giving, and that's what makes it the greatest gift you can give another.

> *To see a world in a grain of sand*
> *And a heaven in a wild flower,*
> *Hold infinity in the palm of your hand*
> *And eternity in an hour.*

William Blake

154

Do not judge or be fearful of what might happen;
do not anticipate the worst. Allow yourself to be
surprised by the present moment.

In what you see let there be only seeing,
in what you hear let there be only hearing.

Buddha

155

As children we all played at being what we wanted to be when we grew up. As adults, there are fewer opportunities for play-acting, because to be a mature adult is to be content with who you are. We may have to let go of the dreams we had as a child and accept the fact that it's OK not to be a superstar. It doesn't mean we have failed. Happiness comes from loving yourself as you are.

When you are discontent, you always want more, more, more. Your desire can never be satisfied. But when you practise contentment, you can say to yourself, 'Oh yes – I already have everything that I really need.'

HH The Dalai Lama

156

Be open to the spirit and awake to the opportunities that await you each day.

I dwell in possibilities.

Emily Dickinson

I visited Israel recently, and I read a lot about the political situation there. Suicide killers are hard to understand, but one thing is sure: to be prepared to do such a dreadful thing, you need to have an enormous passion for your cause.

I went on to wonder, if those of us who are committed to peace had the same level of passion and self-abandonment, the same will and sense of purpose that these killers have, and if we put those energies into building peace, how much might we achieve?

If we cannot end our differences, at least we can help make the world safe for diversity.

John F. Kennedy

158

Growing old is not something that most people look forward to, and it is true that old age may bring health problems and difficulties around losing your independence. But there are blessings too, and with age come growing wisdom, perspective and serenity. So there is no need to deny that you are getting older, or to lie or joke about your age.

The afternoon knows what the
morning never suspected.

Robert Frost

159

Do not anticipate your future based on past experience, because that impoverishes your present and robs it of surprise and novelty. If you do that, you will get quickly bored, like a tourist visiting a place they have already seen in the brochures, seeing nothing new, and finding only what they expect to find.

Our thinking and our behaviour are
always in anticipation of a response.
It is therefore fear-based.

Deepak Chopra

160

When I was a child, I used to watch my mother making bread, and I was fascinated by how the bread soda, just a tiny amount of it, had such an effect on the dough.

I often think of how the smallest act of kindness can make a big difference. You could, of course, make endless lists of all the important things you would like to see changed in the world – the end of earthquakes and tsunamis, wars, atrocities, hunger, unemployment, violence. Some people are called to work for peace and justice, but for the rest of us, the best we can do is try to bring about peace and justice in our small corner. It might not seem much, but like the spoonful of bread soda, even one small act of forgiveness can make a big difference.

One is not born into the world to do
everything but to do something.

Henry David Thoreau

161

I often sat under an old tree in the garden that was planted by my father and grandfather over a hundred years ago. I had the enjoyment of that tree because of their foresight, and because of all the people who worked to keep the garden growing through the years.

It's impossible to imagine how things will be in another hundred years, but at least you can plant seeds for the coming generations – seeds of hope, peace, justice, seeds that may grow into a magnificent future.

*Dream no small dreams for they have
no power to move hearts.*

Johann Wolfgang von Goethe

162

To listen, you need to be quiet, but just to keep
silent is not enough. Listening is not a passive
state but an act: it requires you to hear not only
what is being said but how it is being said.
If you listen closely, you hear also what is not
said. You hear the voice of the soul.

Silence is a source of great strength.

Lao-Tzu

163

Life can be hectic and stressful. You can feel yourself pulled in many directions, and there are so many things going on at once, you can hardly think. At times like this, it is most helpful to remind yourself to be still. If you stop what you are doing, if you let the world race on without you, you give your body, mind and spirit a chance to recuperate. The world will still be there when you're done, but if you take a moment to be still you can re-enter the world more relaxed and with renewed energy.

If water derives lucidity from stillness,
how much more the faculties of the mind!

Chuang Tzu

164

Self-attention or self-focus can lead to greater depression and anxiety: people who are more concerned with themselves and less with others are more likely to feel fearful and unhappy.

Do nothing out of selfish ambition or vain conceit, but in humility consider others better than yourselves.

Philippians 2: 3

165

If your view of life is tired and stale, if everything you see appears empty, maybe it's because you need to be motivated and inspired – refreshed by the world around you. Perhaps the answer lies in seeking out new adventures, or simply looking at the world from a different perspective.

Twenty years from now you will be more disappointed by the things you didn't do than by the ones you did do. So throw off the bowlines, sail away from the safe harbour. Catch the trade winds in your sails. Explore. Dream. Discover.

Mark Twain

166

Deep within you is an amazing inner sanctuary –
the soul. It is a holy place, a Divine place, to
which you may return again and again. A small
voice, the voice of eternity, is heard in your heart,
urging you onward, inviting you to your amazing
destiny, calling you home unto itself.

Behold I am with you always,
even until the end of time.

Matthew 28: 20

Kindness takes many forms. A person kindly calls a friend who is lonely; someone kindly explains a lesson to a student who is having difficulty; a person who has a garden gives vegetables to their neighbour; a kind person smiles at a child waiting in a room full of adults; it can be as simple as holding the door open for a person laden with parcels or pushing a buggy; or as big as devoting your life to working with the poor and the lonely and the hungry.

Kindness is not an act but an attitude, and a kindly attitude can inform even the smallest acts of your life: taking the children to school, going to work, preparing food, answering the phone, sweeping the floor. The most ordinary act can be a kindness if you do it with love.

Kindness is the golden chain by which
society is bound together.

Johann Wolfgang von Goethe

168

Accepting people you meet as they are is a practice that teaches you how not to take things personally and helps you to keep your heart open to possibility rather than tightly shut.

Judgements prevent us from seeing the good that lies beyond appearances.

Wayne Dyer

169

Love begins in your heart, and with every act of kindness, forgiveness, respect, affirmation, appreciation and compassion, you will find it is reinforced and enhanced.

For where your treasure is,
there your heart will be also.

Luke 12: 34

170

To pay attention means to be awake, thus to be aware of what is right in front of you. You might for instance notice a person – that she has black hair, is wearing a shirt and jeans, and looks uncomfortable, as if she hasn't slept well. If you notice that much, the chances are that you are in touch with your feelings and you know how to relate to the person you have observed.

The worst sin towards our fellow
creatures is not to hate them,
but to be indifferent to them.

George Bernard Shaw

171

When we are all taken up with our own thoughts
and worries and desires, our inner world is a
closed system and ultimately oppressive.

You can step out of the closed world of
your own concerns by looking around you,
seeing other people, and choosing to enter their
world.

> *We meet on the broad pathway of good
> faith and good will; no advantage shall be
> taken on either side, but all shall be openness
> and love . . . We are the same as if one man's
> body were to be divided into two parts,
> we are all one flesh and blood.*

William Penn

172

Sometimes, in dark moments, you can feel alone and abandoned. At times like this, a faithful, sensitive friend is a secure shelter and a kindler of light.

It is your joy to find shelter and strength in another in your suffering; and it is your challenge to be that shelter and strength to others, when they in turn need you.

A friendship that makes the least noise is very often the most useful; for which reason I should prefer a prudent friend to a zealous one.

Joseph Addison

Because of the growing mobility of people, we increasingly find ourselves face to face with individuals belonging to other cultures. They have grown up in environments totally different from ours. They have a different religion, a different physical appearance; their customs, food, clothes and attitudes to many things are different.

Your first reaction may be suspicion; racial prejudice has deep roots, and suspicion of others is not a rational reaction that you choose to have. It is an immediate emotional reaction that is beyond your control. Rather than denying that you are prejudiced, face your own prejudice, challenge it and make a rational decision to overcome it.

The man who never alters his opinion is
like standing water, and breeds reptiles of the mind.

William Blake

174

What type of person would you prefer to have to deal with – a proud one or a humble one? Which is likely to be more kind? Or likely to be better company?

If that is the kind of person you like to meet, perhaps it is also the kind of person you might like to be.

> *The fruit of the Spirit is love, joy,*
> *peace, patience, kindness, goodness,*
> *faithfulness, gentleness and self-control.*
> *Against such things there is no law.*

Galatians 5: 22

175

When you have important decisions to make, do so with careful reflection and discernment of heart. If you do that, then you will know that you have made the right decision, and deep inside you, you are at peace.

The truth will set you free.

John 8: 32

176

When you open your heart, God's words challenge you and stir you to action. What word is waiting to be set free in your life? Dare to be open to the call so that it may be spoken with force and dynamism in your life.

The word which God has written
on the brow of every man is hope.

Victor Hugo

177

Immediate gratification is a feature of modern life. We don't want to wait, we want everything straight away, and we become upset, even aggressive, when we cannot have it. We have lost the art of waiting.

To rediscover this art and to teach it to your children is to give them one of the greatest and best possible gifts.

*One moment of patience may
ward off great disaster. One moment of
impatience may ruin a whole life.*

Chinese proverb

178

From a compassionate place, you recognize your own prejudices and biases. Then you can reach out beyond your own circle, with respect and in solidarity, to people of all races and creeds and cultural and economic backgrounds.

Rich and poor have this in common:
The Lord is the Maker of them all.

Proverbs 22: 2

179

Faith is a dance between what is and what could be.

If you have faith as a grain of mustard seed,
you will say to your mountain, 'MOVE!' and it will
move . . . and nothing will be impossible for you.

Matthew 17: 20

180

A story is told about a monastery, where
religious fervour was waning, decadence reigned,
and there was an atmosphere of desperation.
One day a holy man came by and spent some
time with the monks. As he was leaving, he
said, 'Unfortunately I have no advice to give
you, but remember that the Messiah is
among you.'

The monks were astonished by this
revelation and they started to look at each
other in a new way, wondering which one of
them was the Messiah. Was it the lazy one or
the morose one, or the pompous one? Bit by
bit, they started to see each other's faults in
a new light. Perhaps what looked like laziness
was really serenity, moroseness might be a
form of mindfulness; what they had thought
of as pomposity might simply be a kind of

self-esteem. And so, assuming that one of them was the Messiah, they all started to treat each other with a new respect. Relations among the monks were transformed, and so was the whole atmosphere of the community.

Nothing here below is profane
for those who know how to see.
On the contrary,
everything is sacred.

Teilhard de Chardin

Listening

Síle Wall

An ancient wrote: Once upon a time a disciple asked the elder, 'How shall I experience my oneness with creation?'

And the elder answered, 'By listening.'

The disciple pressed the point: 'But how am I to listen?'

And the elder taught, 'Become an ear that pays attention to every single thing the universe is saying. The moment you hear something you yourself are saying, stop.'

Pay attention to everything the universe is saying! As part of planet earth, one small planet in the story of the universe, how can it be possible to pay attention, to adopt a listening ear to all the interconnections that make us part of one universe? And why would we even be interested? The poet Mary Oliver once wrote: 'To pay attention, this is our endless and proper work.[1] In her poem 'Sometimes' she elaborated on this thought. 'Instructions for living a life.[2] Pay attention. Be astonished. Tell about it.' Is this not another way of saying open all sense gates, listen with the eyes, ears, heart and feelings – the whole self? Develop an alert, receptive attitude to the immensity, beauty, incomprehensibility and sacredness of creation, the world you are part of, the universe you belong to? Listen attentively, hear the heartbeat of creation, stay with its pulse and you will move gently into the rhythm of life and find a way of being that is sensitive to all facets of experience – external, internal and contextual?

In your quest to understand the art of attentive listening many voices will come to assist you. But only one is necessary – the voice of silence. There is no listening without the stillness of silence. The art of listening is through silence, listening beyond the sound of words. Listening to the world from within as you become more and more present to yourself.

You say that you are afraid of silence. Embracing silence in today's world is not easy; it is a practice that demands discipline of mind and discipline of body. We tend to run away from silence rather than face nothingness. Never in the history of the world have we been so connected to each other, and so seeking silence requires courage and patience. Getting comfortable with silence is where understanding starts to grow and your capacity to listen will be deepened and transformed: silence is the root of everything. If you spiral into its void, a hundred voices will thunder messages you long to hear.[3]

In this silent space allow yourself time to Pause, Settle, Wait and Listen.

To begin your search take small steps, one at a time. Travel as an explorer, present to yourself while discovering something new with each step. Your pathway will invariably be different from someone else's journey. Notice the subtleties of change that occur moment by moment. Listen with your heart for those once-in-a-while fleeting sacred moments, moments that bring life. See how each day offers multidimentional opportunities to pause and listen. Grow into your experience. The language of silence will invite you to see little things as important metaphors in your quest.

The following are some suggestions that you might find helpful as a way of moving deeper along this journey of discovery.

Awaken early: experience that moment of change when night and day intermingle and merge, when darkness and light become one. Pause. Settle. Wait. Listen.

Go to the countryside or visit a park: experience the changing seasons – Spring becoming Summer, Autumn becoming Winter – light changing, shadows lengthening, shadows shortening. Dying and rising, the earthly cycle of each year. Pause. Settle. Wait. Listen and discover.

Sit by the ocean and allow the expanse and vastness of the horizon to invite you into its never-ending rhythm of becoming, the rhythm of life. Discover silence, engage with it.

> *Listen to the whisper of moonlight on the water,*
> *Close your eyes and listen.*
> *Listen to the singing of the feather on the breeze,*
> *Close your eyes and listen.* [4]

Each day brings its own reality. You read, hear and experience stories of war and bloodshed, violence and oppression, poverty and injustice, murder and suicide; of human rights being violated. It is difficult to tune into sorrow and grief if you have been deaf to its place in your own life. Discover the vulnerabilities in your own life; don't resist them or they will just become noise, a noise that shuts you out from living life. Take the first step.

Engage with your vulnerability, embrace it, allow yourself the time and space to fully absorb its significance as you connect lovingly with it in the silence of your heart, and you will know 'that the soul exists and is built entirely out of attentiveness'.[5] You will discover that self-awareness becomes a treasure worth finding in your quest to understand the art of attending to another, the art of listening. To listen and respond to human pain calls for a special quality of attention, a listening that allows the feelings, the unspoken words, find a home in you.

'To listen to another person into a condition of disclosure is the greatest service you can bestow on another human being.'[6] To really listen beyond the outer layer of words that are spoken will bring you into the depth of mystery, that place where heart connects with heart. It is a creative process stemming from your understanding and experience within the stillness of silence.

May your listening be attuned
To the deeper silence
Where sound is honed
To bringing distance home.[7]

In your quest to be a person of presence, begin just where you are, attentive to yourself as a bodily being living in a moment of time. Attentiveness will make you fully alive. Attentive listening will make you fully alive to the world you are part of. The art of listening only comes through the power of silence. Listening to the noise within that needs quieting and the wisdom from outside that needs to be learned. Active listening asks that you still the activity of your mind, become more present to yourself, take time just to be in and live each day mindfully, moment by moment, by moment.

Silence will then take you on a journey and on that journey you will discover that 'it is with the heart that one really sees'.[8] It is with the heart that you will truly hear. Silence is the meeting place. Be the silence that is needed when someone else speaks:

'Whenever there is some silence around you – listen to it. That means just notice it. Pay attention to it. Listening to silence awakens the dimension of stillness within yourself, because it is only through stillness that you can be aware of silence'.[9]

Engaging with creation – silence
Becoming one with creation – stillness
The art of listening beyond words – life

[1] 'To pay attention . . .': from Mary Oliver, 'Yes! No!' in *Owls and Other Fantasies: Poems and Essays*, Beacon Press, Boston, 2003, p. 27.

[2] 'Instructions for living a life': from 'Sometimes', in Mary Oliver's 2008 collection, *Red Bird*, Beacon Press, 2009.

[3] Jalaluddin Rumi, a thirteenth-century Persian poet and Sufi mystic with worldwide recognition.

[4] 'Listen', recorded by Christy Moore, was written by Hank Wedell from Mallow, Co. Cork, and the song appears on the album *Listen* on the Columbia label at Sony Music.

[5] Mary Oliver, 'Low tide', *Amicus Journal*, Winter 2001, p. 34.

[6] Jean Vanier, *Becoming Human*, Dartom, Longman and Todd, London, 1998.

[7] John O'Donohue, 'For the Senses', in *To Bless The Space Between Us: A Book of Blessings* by John O'Donohue, Doubleday, 2008.

[8] Antoine de Saint-Exupéry, *The Little Prince* (1943), Chapter 21.

[9] Eckhart Tolle, *Stillness Speaks: Whispers of Now*, Hodder Mobius, 2003.

181

Attention is the medium through which kindness
flows. Without attention, there is no kindness
and no empathy and no relationships.

*It is only when we give complete attention
to a problem, and solve it immediately – never
carrying it over to the next day, the next minute – that
there is solitude. To have inward solitude and
space is very important because it implies freedom
to be, to go, to function, to fly.*

Krishnamurti

182

When you are relaxed, you don't react to forces that are out of your control. Instead, you can choose to put your energy into what you can control.

So relax.

How beautiful it is to do nothing,
and then to rest afterwards.

Spanish proverb

183

Imagination is your greatest gift, for it allows you to participate in the act of creation itself.

Imagination is not a talent of some men,
but is the health of every man.

Ralph Waldo Emerson

184

We are all called to be peacemakers, but peacemaking is of little value to someone who is dying of hunger or cold. It will not remove the pain of torture; it will not make an impression on anyone who is treated as an alien. Neither will it comfort the loved ones of people who are murdered or raped.

Peacemaking is only real and valuable when the peacemaker is aware of the rampant injustice and violence in the world, until he or she examines their own participation in violence and injustice and identifies non-violently with the oppressed and the suffering.

Keep in mind those who are in prison, as though you were in prison with them; and those who are badly treated, since you too are in the one body.

Hebrews 13: 3

What is it about driving that makes people so
stubborn and aggressive? I witnessed a scene
on a country road in Ireland. The road was too
narrow for two cars to pass each other, and the
only thing that could be done was for one driver
to give way to the oncoming car, reverse, pull
in, and let the other car pass. Usually, the
system worked, but on this occasion neither
driver wanted to give way. They stopped and
confronted each other. Both insisted they had
right of way. The more they insisted, the less
either of them was inclined to yield. Traffic
started to back up behind them, and still they
would not stop arguing.

There were no winners in that situation.
Both the drivers wasted time, both were probably
late for their appointments, wherever they were
going, both probably arrived, eventually, angry

and upset and with their blood pressure through the roof, and on top of that they made everyone else on the road late and angry too.

A little co-operation saves a lot of conflict – and time.

We all do better when we work together.
Our differences do matter,
but our common humanity matters more.

Bill Clinton

186

In the Celtic tradition, times where the two worlds meet – the divine and the earthly – are called 'thin places', and twilight is one such 'thin place'.

Mary Aikenhead, founder of my own order, the Religious Sisters of Charity, loved sunset and twilight. She wrote of how she found the hour of sundown with the beauty of the night moving towards her a constant consolation during long illness.

The sun knows when it's time for setting.

Psalm 104: 19

187

You cannot always be conscious of the Divine presence, but you can dedicate your heart to God so that always and everywhere, even when you are at work or at play and concentrating on other things, the spirit prays in you.

I live – now not I –
but Christ lives in me.

Galatians 2:20

188

Love is risky, but it is also transforming; it turns the most horrific situations into beauty and light.

Love must be as much a light, as it is a flame.

Henry David Thoreau

189

A person who tries to show how clever they are cannot be truly kind, for their kindness will be condescending. Only a humble person can be kind, for they are not playing one-upmanship games; they are not trying to get the better of another person, or gain the advantage over someone.

A great man is always willing to be little.

Ralph Waldo Emerson

190

An adventure is by definition a new and risky experience. It demands energy, trust and commitment. It is a means of moving into the unknown.

At any time on any given day, you don't know what possibilities lie ahead, how far you are into an adventure or how it will end. But you should know that you are not alone in your adventure.

> *Somewhere, something incredible is*
> *waiting to be known.*
>
> Blaise Pascal

191

Your vision is, no doubt, often shrouded by a fog
of uncertainty, as the mountains are before dawn.
But if you rest in the ambiguity and allow the
spirit to lead you through the doubt and the fear
to a new sense of purpose, then the light can
break in, the sun can come forth, revealing and
rekindling the fire burning in the heart of who
you are.

*When Jesus spoke again to the people,
he said, 'I am the light of the world.
Whoever follows me will never walk in darkness,
but will have the light of life.'*

John 8: 12

192

According to the World Health Organization, poverty is the world's greatest killer. It says: *Poverty wields its destructive influence at every stage of human life, from the moment of conception to the grave.*

Your challenge is to join your voice in loud protest over the unequal distribution of resources and the disproportionate degree of suffering that is endured by the poor. That is your call, to stand with your suffering sisters and brothers and take a strong position against injustice, poverty and oppression.

An injustice anywhere
is an injustice everywhere.

Samuel Johnson

193

Kindness and compassion are a source of lasting happiness and joy, the foundation of a loving heart.

If you want others to be happy, practise compassion.
If you want to be happy, practise compassion.

HH The Dalai Lama

194

People think a good salesperson is a good talker, but a really good salesperson listens to what the customer wants. Being a good listener also helps you to be a good parent or a good spouse, a good neighbour and a good friend.

Listen not merely to what is said
but to the tone of voice in which it is said.

Chinese proverb

195

Life is created when you trust in the promise of unseen things, just as buds hold life in the depth of winter.

Those who trust us educate us.

George Eliot

196

You carry darkness within you. You have shadows that need attention: your fears, your memories, your grudges. Every war is inside you and me, and only you and I can stop what causes the war within us.

If you turn your light inwardly,
you will find what is esoteric within you.

Hui Neng

197

Hope opens your heart to possibility.

When the world says, 'Give up,'
Hope whispers, 'Try it one more time.'

Anonymous

198

If you are insensitive to the emotions of others,
your relationships become a charade.

If you see other people not as people but as
commodities – things on a par with your fridge or
your car – you may start to allow yourself to
manipulate and even to violate them.

Don't walk behind me, I may not lead.
Don't walk in front of me, I may not follow.
Just walk beside me and be my friend.

Anonymous

199

Insecure people are not content to be what they are and who they are, they are busy trying to prove they are better than others, and that becomes their purpose in life.

Do not waste time trying to be what you are not. Rather, permit yourself to be who you are.

Then God looked over all He had made
And He saw that it was very good.

Genesis 1: 31

200

Every frightening situation offers you a chance to grow. Strength comes from experiencing and over-coming your fears, not from hiding away from them. Working through your problems teaches you how to deal with problems you may have in the future.

Fear and courage are brothers.

Proverb

201

No matter how much you think you know what is best for other people, what is really best for them is for them to work out for themselves. You have enough mistakes of your own to make and mend.

When one intends to move or speak,
one should first examine one's own mind and
then act appropriately with composure.

Shantideva

202

Resentment is a barrier to your growth.
Forgiveness is the beginning of your freedom.

> *'I can forgive but I cannot forget' is only
> another way of saying I cannot forgive.*

Henry Ward Beecher

203

Stand ready to receive joy when it is given. Accept
its absence when it is not.

> *Miracles come in moments. Be ready and willing.*

Wayne Dyer

204

A newborn child cries in the presence of other crying babies. Bit by bit, empathy develops and becomes the capacity to understand other people's feelings and points of view, to identify with them.

If you can empathize with others, your existence is immeasurably richer and varied. You can step out of yourself and into the lives of others. Relationships become a source of interest and of emotional and spiritual nourishment.

*To touch the soul of another human being
is to walk on holy ground.*

Stephen Covey

205

Stillness gives you serenity and choice.

*Our responsibility is no longer
to acquire, but to be.*

Rabindranath Tagore

206

When you pay attention to another human being, you offer nourishment and you are close to them. You give your presence and your love from your heart.

*Only love can bring human beings to their
perfect completion as individuals, by uniting
them one with another, because only love
takes possession of them and unites
them by what lies deepest within them.*

Teilhard de Chardin

207

Apathy is a most destructive force. Perhaps you don't like to be inconvenienced, or you don't like to be moved beyond your comfort zone, and so you stick to what you know, what is familiar.

But what you don't know is vast and wonderful, and if you don't commit the time and energy to discover and study the universe, you are missing life's endless opportunities.

To dare is to lose one's footing momentarily.
To not dare is to lose oneself.

Søren Kierkegaard

208

You can only love someone in the present. For all your relationships, the only time is now.

Being deeply loved by someone gives you strength, while loving someone deeply gives you courage.

Lao-Tzu

209

Adversity is good. It shows you your limits, teaches you how much anger you can handle, how to take care of yourself and how to be independent.

Love your enemies,
for they will tell you your faults.

Benjamin Franklin

210

Living in the now challenges your tendency to
wait or delay until success is assured before
beginning.

Rejoice in the things that are
present; all else is beyond thee.

Montaigne

211

Knowledge and understanding will give you
rational explanations for all manner of things. But
it is only imagination that can take you away beyond
the known, to the mystery of today and tomorrow.

It is pointless to try to shape the
world to fit our desires:
we must transform our minds.

Matthieu Ricard

212

If you believe you are created in love and that you live in Divine love, then when you love, the possibilities are infinitely greater than anything you can imagine. No loving thought, word or action escapes the effect.

*Let us love one another
since love comes from God.*

1 John 4: 7

213

Knowing a person's story softens your judgement and makes you more tolerant, and that leads to peace. So take the time to listen to what people tell you about themselves.

*Wisdom is the reward you get
for a lifetime of listening when
you'd have preferred to talk.*

Doug Larson

214

First you pray, then you wait. You wait in the darkness, you wait in silence, you wait and listen in love.
And you discover that your soul has eyes that can
see in the dark and ears that can hear in the silence.

See with the heart. Listen with the soul. And
you will find a new way of being: an answer to prayer.

*We have more possibilities available in
each moment than we realize.*

Thich Nhat Hanh

215

If you are aware of your strengths as well as your weaknesses, then you don't need to flaunt how clever you are, and you don't need to triumph in order to justify your existence. You can accept that other people are better than you at some things, just as you too have your special gifts.

The unexamined life
is not worth living.

Socrates

216

If conflicts arise between you and someone you love, you deal best with them not by daydreaming, but by being awake.

It takes two to quarrel,
but only one to end it.

Spanish proverb

217

Dare to trust, and let God be God.

When you are weak, God makes you strong. When you are powerless, God's power comes to you.

All you have to do is trust.

God's gifts put man's
best dreams to shame.

Elizabeth Barrett Browning

218

From the moment of your birth, you are dependent on the care and kindness of others. Later in life, when you face the suffering and illness of old age, you are again dependent on the kindness of others.

   At the beginning and at the end of life, you depend on others' kindness, and in the middle you have your opportunity to act kindly towards others. Take it, and be grateful that you have a chance to make a difference to another person's life.

How wonderful that no one
need wait a single moment
to improve the world.

Anne Frank

219

In Bertolucci's famous film, *The Last Emperor*, a royal child is brought up to believe he is a god. He lives in a magnificent palace, and he is served and honoured as the centre of the universe. Then come great upheavals, the social structure crumbles, and there is a sudden end to all his privileges. The emperor, forced to flee his palace, comes to realize that he is human, not superior to others but equal, a man like others, subject to pain and uncertainty.

By humbling himself, he discovers who he is: his is not a defeat, but an unexpected victory.

The Sage knows what is in him,
but makes no display; he respects himself,
but seeks not honour for himself.

Lao-Tzu

With Mirth and Laughter Let Old Wrinkles Come

Lelia Doolan

John O'Donohue was a poetic and prophetic thinker. His sudden death at the age of fifty-two was the sudden forfeit of an unforgettable friend and of the balm of robust and vivid encounters with him. One of the great echoes of these meetings was his laugh.

It was a huge event, starting somewhere in the subterranean regions below his tall frame, working its way upwards like an impatient geyser, barely ever held in check until finally exploding into peals and paeans of rolling rousing paroxysms that threatened to burst buttons and split coat seams; rumbling and roaring across rooms, out windows, scattering small birds, rustling through branches, rousing the world in street and field, dancing across bog and stone mountain. It infected all to their betterment.

I thought that this laughter was all his own until I heard his mother Josie, now also among the dear shades. She was the living model for this mighty engine of hilarity and she passed it on not only to him but to his sister and brothers. It will probably go on cascading for ever in my mind, along with the many great bundles of new jokes he gathered up from the same brothers.

And was always ready to recount.

A man came to this small village to live. He did not know much about country life. He decided to raise pigs. When the pigs were reared, he began bringing them to market. He carried them in his arms, one at a time. On his way, he met his neighbour, an experienced farming man. The neighbour watched this laborious journey in and out to the market, one pig at a time in the man's arms. Finally he said:

'Why are you carrying those pigs yourself, one at a time? Wouldn't you get a cart to put them all in?'

'Why would I do that?' asked your man.

'Well, for one thing,' said the farmer, 'it would save a lot of time.'

'Oh, I see. But no, you're all right. Sure, what's time to a pig?'

*

Pat, John's brother, told this story at his funeral mass. It was one of John's favourite stories about notions of time. I later heard a personal variation of it from the late great wildlife film-maker, Eamon de Buitléar. Perhaps it is true, as another philosopher said. 'I know why it is man alone who laughs; he alone suffers so deeply that he had to invent laughter.' I have seen dogs and cats smile, and even the odd cow, but I have never heard them laugh. Maybe I am not on their wavelength.

There's also the story, or maybe many stories, about how someone with serious cancer had a long remission after watching Marx Brothers' films, and Buster Keaton's, Charlie Chaplin's, Laurel and Hardy's. He made a fine recovery after nearly dying of laughter. More good muscles are involved in laughing than in weeping, it seems.

I never heard of anyone being cured by laughing out loud at the stories in the Old Testament. But Woody Allen once remarked: 'If you want to make God laugh, tell him your plans.'

Without death and disaster (preferably not your own) would there ever have been any antidote, sauce or drollery or witty resistance to the mutilations of daily life? How did it all begin? Did some early human lose his balance and fall out of an old bush in the Olduvai Gorge and a fellow traveller saw it and guffawed, punctuating the moment, maybe puncturing the gymnast's ego? I'd see laughter as a percussive instrument, like the drum and rhythm section of life. It can fracture the flatline of good old dull everyday moments. It can turn the expected upside down, like shaking the landscape in a kaleidoscope. Giving a new perspective.

One rainy day, a man was driving his car along an unfamiliar road. He came to a dip in the road where there was a large pool of water with a man sitting on the wall beside it.

'I wonder,' the driver called out to this observer, as he drew up: 'can I get through here or is it too deep for the car?'

'You're grand; you'll get through easy,' said the native on the wall. Off went the driver in his car and got completely swamped in the middle of the flood.

'What do you mean, get through easy?' he yelled.

'I can't understand that at all,' said my weather eye, 'a duck went past here a minute ago and' – holding his hand up to his chest – 'it only came up to here on him!' And he laughed so much he fell off the wall.

The driver's laughter is not reported. So, does the victor laugh more than the victim? Laughter triumphant or laughter defensive that tries to cover the hurt? I don't know. I'd like to think of us as playful beings who try to treat oppression, poverty, imprisonment, humiliation, with the respectful gallows humour of our derision. Which we mostly do. But there is plenty of the other, as well. The actor Micheál MacLiammóir, asked to name the chief characteristic of the Irish, said: 'Malice!' South Dubliners are well used to treating north Dubliners or Kerrymen as laughable dolts – just as the Poles or the Irishmen in British jokes are supposed to feel the barb of their perceived inferiority. Even though laughing at jokes is only one small reason for laughter.

I once had a very enjoyable and funny weekend in London, hearing and laughing with the contagious humour of a Buddhist teacher discussing the Tibetan Book of the Dead. It reminded me of Ginny Gogan, the shrewd, penniless little mother of many children 'born between the borders of the Ten Commandments', in Sean O'Casey's play *The Plough and the Stars*. Mrs Gogan is addicted to visions of death. One of these must be at the heart of all wry laughter: she finds herself having a kind of forbidden joy 'to be movin' along in a mourning coach', thinking that maybe the next funeral will be her own but 'glad, in a quiet way, that this is somebody else's'. It was in tune with O'Casey's dedication of the play: *to the gay laugh of my mother at the gate of the grave*. And it suggests to me that without death, there might well be no need at all for laughter.

Which brings me to wonder at what different cultures and belief systems find droll. Do Italians and Kenyans, Muslims and Chileans, Japanese and Jews laugh at the same things? Are there underlying and universal experiences which touch all funny bones? Not all jokes are worth laughing at; many comedians are glum by nature. That's the paradox. And some of the Sufi teaching stories about a holy fool like, say, the Mulla Nasrudin, convey mysterious and astonishing truths under the guise of a crazy wiliness. He is trickster, beggar and sage. His disarming directness seems to embody a delightful childish relish.

The Mulla went to see a rich man:

'Give me some money.'

'Why?'

'I want to buy . . . an elephant.'

'If you have no money, you can't afford to keep an elephant.'

'I came here,' said Nasrudin, 'to get money, not advice.'

*

It sounds dotty. Like the kind of story a child would tell. Children chuckle all the time. They don't seem to have to smile first – they can break into happy shrieking and giggling without any practice at all. They could teach us to let that impatient geyser escape in hilarious howls of jollity.

As Mr Shakespeare had it: with mirth and laughter let old wrinkles come.

220

Risk-taking belongs not only to the strong and the powerful. If you let free your creative spirit within and dare to risk, you will discover that you are capable of much more than you ever dreamed of.

I dip my pen in the blackest ink,
because I'm not afraid of falling into my inkpot.

Ralph Waldo Emerson

221

You create the beauty and wonder of your life just by living.

Love is the beauty of the soul.

St Augustine of Hippo

222

You have probably been educated to believe that you are an individual with well-defined boundaries. You may believe that the way to live is to roll up your sleeves and get cracking in order to improve yourself and produce something worthwhile.

This is all well and good, but sometimes this way of thinking leads people to think they owe nothing to anyone. That's a false idea.

You are not a separate individual, surrounded by other separate individuals; you are not responsible only for yourself and your own production. You are more like a cell with a permeable membrane, and you live by continuous exchange with others, you depend on other cells for your life.

The way we communicate with others and with ourselves
ultimately determines the quality of our lives.

Anthony Robbins

223

When you are confined to your own thoughts,
worries and desires you are closed.

If you can step out of this inner world and
enter the worlds of other people's passions, fears,
hopes and sufferings, you will come to view your
own concerns with more objectivity, and you will
be healthier and happier.

*We take the limits of our own vision
for the limits of the world.*

Arthur Schopenhauer

224

If you devote yourself to competing with others, you'll have less energy for what really counts: for learning and for creating, for rapport with others, for being open to a world full of opportunities. So forget about comparisons; be yourself, and you will not only find a new freedom, but you will also gain a whole world of opportunity.

If you would create something, you must be something.

Johann Wolfgang von Goethe

225

Where gratitude is open and intimate, life becomes easier. You are no longer anxious to prove yourself. You stop complaining. You discover that happiness is already here, it already exists, unsuspected, right in front of your eyes.

The ego can only be erased through happiness and gratitude.

Arnaud Desjardins

226

Sometimes, you have only wordless words. Those times, you just have to trust.

He who trusts in himself is lost,
he who trusts in God can do all things.

St Alphonsus Liguori

227

Listening brings relief to the listener as well as to the person who tells. To listen, you have to empty yourself of yourself. While you listen to the other, your own troubles and anxieties do not exist. While you are listening, you are free. Your inner noise is quietened. Peace descends on you.

Let your heart guide you.
It whispers softly, so listen closely.

Anonymous

228

Every morning, you have a choice about how to approach your day. If you greet the day by deciding to see the best in people and events, you can create an atmosphere of joy and goodwill wherever you go.

What a wonderful gift to give to yourself and others when you choose to bring brightness and happiness to other people's lives!

Happiness is not something ready made.
It comes from your own actions.

HH The Dalai Lama

229

A quarrel where neither party has the least intention of seeing things from the other's point of view is doomed never to end. It's the same thing in international relations. Accepting the other is what would most help to resolve age-old racial and cultural prejudices, and yet it is what is most often missing.

From a worldly point of view,
there is no mistake so great as that
of being always right.

Samuel Butler

If mindless speed is somebody running around an airport, shouting into a mobile phone, then moving mindfully is walking through a garden with a three-year-old, noticing everything the child is noticing.

If you move mindfully, you have time to question and time to listen to the answers before moving on. When you move mindfully, it occurs to you to wonder where God is leading and calling you in the midst of the plans you have for yourself.

*Actions may be positive or negative
according to the intention that underlies
them, just as a crystal refracts the
colours of its surroundings.*

Dilgo Khyentse Rinpoche

Who are you?

You know who you have been – you remember your past, your background, your experience – but there is more of you still waiting to be realized if you have the courage to let it be, to trust and to let go of the familiar.

To grow to your potential, you have to stay connected to the source of Divine love and inspiration.

*We must make good use of this life
for the time that we have left, this
brief flash of light, like the sun
appearing through the clouds.*

Kalu Rinpoche

232

Moses led his people to new life. In an act of faith, he pointed to the new place where his people would find peace.

Did he know for sure where he was leading them, because he had seen it? No, but his trust was in the holy one, in the one he met in prayer.

In your time, you too are called to be a discoverer of new lands, created for you. Have faith.

Call to me and I will answer you
and tell you great and unsearchable
things you do not know.

Jeremiah 33: 3

233

No virtue is really a virtue unless it's permeated and informed by love. For example, justice without love is legalism. Hope without love is self-centredness. Care without love is duty. Service without love is servitude. Every virtue is an expression of love.

Life is a challenge, meet it!
Life is a dream, realize it!
Life is a game, play it!
Life is Love, enjoy it!

Sri Sathya Sai Baba

234

Walking in the woods one day, I came across the trunk of an old, old tree. It had been cut down some time ago, possibly because it was decayed or maybe it had been battered by storms. Moss had begun to grow on it and over it and young sprouts rose out of its cracks and tatters. This fallen tree reminded me of the way life sometimes works out for us.

Don't be disappointed if your hopes have not been realized; your plans may look dead to you, but even during the darkest days there are endless possibilities waiting for you. You just have to look closely enough to see them.

The seed of God is in us.
The seed of the pear tree grows into a pear tree.
The seed of the hazel grows into a hazel.
And the seed of God grows into God.

Meister Eckhart

235

Listening to what others have to say should not be considered a boring duty but an interesting adventure. If you really listen, you will find that everyone has something interesting to say – even the person who appears most ordinary. Try it and see!

It is the province of knowledge
to speak, and it is the privilege
of wisdom to listen.

Oliver Wendell Holmes

236

One of the most important things to learn is that you can make a difference in life. What you do matters.

When you believe that, you can move into this moment with courage and the ability to face all the challenges that come.

The hour is striking so close above me,
so clear and sharp,
that all my senses ring with it.
I feel it now, there's a power in me
to grasp and give shape to my world.

Rainer Maria Rilke

237

When the little birds sing and chirp in greeting to the sun, who is to say that they are not giving thanks to the sun for coming with light and happiness to free them from the cold of the night? It is our stinginess in giving that makes us reluctant to admit that gratitude in animals may be deeper than our own.

> *I hear beyond the range of sound,*
> *I see beyond the range of sight,*
> *New earths and skies and seas abound,*
> *And in my day the sun doth pale his light.*

Henry David Thoreau

A woman came to visit me once who had had a very difficult life. She had been abused by her father at a very young age and quickly found herself homeless and exploited, a victim of prostitution. She was now trying to find her place in the world.

She was sent to me by someone in Focus Ireland who worked with homeless people. In describing her meeting with this person, the woman explained to me why she had trusted him: 'He looked at me and spoke to me as no other man had ever done in my life.'

In spite of all her terrible experiences, the woman recognized the face of love when she saw it.

Have the courage to trust love one more time,
and always one more time.

Maya Angelou

239

Things do not always go according to plan. If you are moving along at a great speed, believing you are in control, even a traffic light delay can be interpreted as a personal affront rather than a neutral event.

If, on the other hand, you choose to surrender to surprise, you'll find you are much less anxious, more in control of your life.

The secret to humour is surprise.

Aristotle

240

Judging other people as soon as you meet them, or even when you just see them on the street or on the bus or at a social event, is quick and easy, it costs nothing, and it gives you a false sense of superiority over the other person. Whether your judgement is accurate or faulty, it will interfere with the potential new relationship. The other person will feel it and be influenced by it, and possibly be hurt or offended by it.

Respect, on the other hand, is the full acknowledgement of yourself and of other people. It means giving to others the space they deserve, rather than leaping to hasty conclusions and judging harshly.

Men are respectable only as they respect.

Ralph Waldo Emerson

241

If you open your ears, you can listen to the words that are being spoken to you.

If you open your eyes, you can see the new movement of this moment.

If you open your heart, you can shape this day to respond to those who will cross your path.

Thou that hast given so much to me,
give one thing more, a grateful heart.

George Herbert

242

It is by understanding and accepting your own weaknesses that you become truly human. This is your reality, this is how you truly are, and that is a solid base from which you can humbly make contact with other people.

Every morning, our first thought should be a wish to devote the day to the good of all living beings.

Dilgo Khyentse Rinpoche

243

It can feel good to be around people who are humble, who are careful and compassionate; these people possess a rare form of serenity that only humility can yield.

Humility is the solid foundation of all virtues.

Kong Fu Zi

There is an organization called L'Arche which cares with great love and tenderness for people with disabilities. If a person leaves the care of L'Arche for any reason, the organization continues to be loyal to that person. They say, 'We carry them in our hearts.'

To hold a person in your heart is to take a consistent interest in them, to treat them with respect, without judging them, so that they know you are on their side, and will always be there for them. The essence of such a friendship is loyalty.

*Wisdom and compassion should
become the dominating influences that guide
our thoughts, our words, and our actions.*

Matthieu Ricard

245

At the centre of your being there is a core of truth. This is what compels you to take a stand on an issue where you know an injustice is being done, to follow your conscience, to put yourself on the line for the truth, no matter what the consequences may be.

You cannot be at peace in your heart of hearts when you deviate from that truth and when you are not in right relationships with yourself, with others, with society and with creation.

Wisdom is found only in truth.

Johann Wolfgang von Goethe

246

You come to this moment with the experience that has made you who you are. You come with a hope that all things are possible. With the strength of the spirit given to you, you know you can make a difference.

*The forces which move the cosmos
are no different from those which
move the human soul.*

Lama Anagarika Govinda

247

Speed tends to cancel out peace. When you move at speed, you are out of touch with Spirit and when you are out of touch with Spirit, the ego steps in and takes control. Slow down!

*We are always getting ready to live,
but never living.*

Ralph Waldo Emerson

The founder of Buddhism was once asked to present a talk on truth to his followers. But instead of talking, he took a flower from a nearby vase and gazed at it.

Everyone was puzzled by his behaviour, but, suddenly, one person smiled. He understood the point the Buddha was making: words are just words; reality lies in being, not in thinking or speaking.

Without the rigidity of concepts, the world becomes transparent and illuminated, as though lit from within. With this understanding, the interconnectedness of all that lives becomes very clear.

Sharon Salzberg

Faith is a gift; not one to be hoarded, but one to be shared.

It is important to respect other people's personal convictions, but that doesn't mean you should be reluctant to share your faith with others, in your words, your example, your interest and your sense of conviction and dedication.

> *To one who has faith,*
> *no explanation is necessary.*
> *To one without faith,*
> *no explanation is possible.*

St Thomas Aquinas

250

You have your own vineyard, but you are also joined to your neighbour's vineyard, without any dividing lines. The vineyards are so joined together that you cannot do good or evil for yourself without doing the same for your neighbour.

*The universal power that manifests
itself in the universal law
is at one with our true power.*

Rabindranath Tagore

251

When the great social activist Daniel Bergin was asked about his work, his marches, his protests for peace, all of which seemed to be in vain, he replied, 'We are all called to be faithful, not to be successful.'

Most of the work you do for justice may not be successful, but if you concentrate not on the results but on the value of the work itself, you will know that fidelity and goodness will always triumph.

If we really believe in something,
we have no choice, have we,
but to go further.

Graham Greene

252

Mystery draws you deep into the darkness of not knowing, and that space is lonely. No one can enter into the uniqueness of your experience, even those who are very close to you. You stutter and stumble in the presence of mystery: of a sunset, a friendship, a star.

If the works of God were such as might be easily comprehended by human reason, they could not be called wonderful or unspeakable.

Thomas à Kempis

253

The ability to see value in a humble or unremarkable situation is essential for happiness and well-being. If you concentrate not on what you have but on what you lack, what you still want, you will never be happy. Happiness consists in being able to appreciate what others take for granted: a fine day, a smile, good health.

As we express our gratitude,
we must never forget that the highest
appreciation is not to utter words,
but to live by them.

John F. Kennedy

Soul

Brother Richard Hendrick

God created man in His image;
in the Divine image He created Him;
male and female He created them.
Genesis 1: 27

The Lord God formed man out of the clay of the ground
and blew into his nostrils the breath of life,
and so man became a living Soul.
Genesis 2: 7

Nowadays, Soul can often be seen as a word that deadens with its weight, rather than as an experience that vivifies with its presence. In Hebrew, the root language of the tradition to which I belong, there are two basic words used to describe the different parts of what we call soul: *nephesh* and *ruach*. They mean very different things, but neither exists fully without the other to define it; and in the dance of their relationship we come close to discovering the unique and ancient insights that, when received fully, allow our understanding of what Soul is to become utterly transformative and liberating.

However, before we get to the inner meaning of Soul, we must abandon some concepts about our souls that too many of us hold without ever having examined them fully. They are a hangover from that period we call the 'Enlightenment', when soul and body were tragically separated with a Cartesian knife, an injury that has yet to be healed in the psyche of the West. Because of this philosophical butchering, when asked to describe what a soul is, the majority of us descend into images of ghosts inhabiting bodies. We speak of 'having a soul' in the same way that we have a dog, or a father or a job. It is almost as though we imagine that just as if we lost our pet, our parent or our employment, we should still exist independently (though saddened by the loss we have endured); so if we lost our soul, we should be fine, if a little less 'full'. Of course, nothing could be further from the truth. As the great C. S. Lewis was wont to remind his pupils, 'You do not have a soul, you are a soul.' The 'I' that you are (beyond and deeper than the mere egoistic I); the individual expression of Divine creativity that is your unique presence in the world; this is your soul. The You-ness of you is the apprehension of your soul by your intellect. So what is this Soul-stuff that we are? For that we must go back to the very beginning again . . . to the dance of *nephesh* with *ruach*, of inbreath and outbreath . . .

In the Book of Genesis we are told in the most magnificent poetry just what it is we are. (We are the subject of poem and myth, all of it true, for the simple reason that myth and poem speak to our souls in ways that the dry digest of history never will.) So what are we told there? Simply that our life is the result of Divine inspiration: we have been breathed awake. We ARE a living soul by virtue of this Divine inbreathing. We may live this earthly life, as the Chinese sages say, between the inbreath of birth and the outbreath of our passing, but we began as humanity through a Divine Exhalation which granted life and movement and awareness of our relationship with God, with one another and with creation. The mud-moulded mannequin of the pagan myths awakens to its true nature in the Hebrew revelation that we are not that which perishes and dies; rather we are that which is called to respond to the Creator as Father/Lover for eternity. The soul that is breathed into the 'man' is the *nephesh*, the creative power of God. It is not God, but, as the ancient monks and Hebrew mystics will realize through their inward encounter, it is a Divine energy proceeding from God and holding us in being. As we breathe we are held in the sustaining breath of God. We are ensouled by Divine breath, by Divine Life itself. God bestows the gift of *nephesh*, our individual personhood; our soul. Mind, heart and personality arise from the *nephesh*. So that there would be no mistake about the intimate and unique relationship that humankind enjoys, through its soul, with its creator, the ancient Hebrew sages and prophets went further and coined the word *ruach* to speak of the Divine indwelling at the heart of the Soul. This is the utterly unique spark of presence, by which we are connected to God at the heart of our being. *Ruach* is the indwelling Spirit of God, the activity of God within us. The *ruach* of God dwells within us as the Spirit of God dwelt in the Temple. The One who hovered over the waters of primordial chaos and called forth order, harmony and beauty hovers too within the depths of *nephesh*, within the depths of our soul, in that place we call Spirit, and, if yielded to, will call us into order, peace and harmony also. It is through allowing the action of the *ruach* of God within that the image and likeness of God is gradually seen without. An image that as we see from the scripture above will be called forth from every human being regardless of gender, creed or colour.

So how do we come to know our soul? How do we

yield to the action of the *ruach*, the Spirit of God within us; such that our *nephesh* may grow and the image of God be revealed within us and so within the world? The answer is surprisingly simple . . . perhaps too simple. It has been known since the beginning of time, but through the egoistic amnesia that we call sin it is forgotten time and time again and must be relearned by the sages, the prophets, the monks and the mystics so that they may wake us anew to the full beauty of what we are in our essence. The answer is simply to breathe . . . to breathe in a way that unites awareness with deep stillness and attentiveness, to watch what arises within and to cling to what is good while letting all that is not fall away from us. To align our breath with the Divine inbreathing is to align our being with Divine presence. It is to enter the sacred desert within where even the bushes burn with the revelation of the God who IS, 'Yahweh', the great 'I AM'. The One whose very name invites us to find Him in the present moment where we anchor ourselves in the soul-space of breath.

'God is breath,' said the great St Maximos the Confessor, one of those who, like Elijah the prophet before him, went into the desert to discover the revelation that comes to those who persevere in stillness. They are those who sit in the cave of the heart until the storms and the hurricanes, the earthquakes and the fires, of our emotions and desires have risen and blown themselves out. For then they behold within themselves the revelation of the *ruach* of the Spirit of God who comes to the one who stills themselves and who has learned the inner art of Soul listening, like a still small voice, a gentle murmuring breath, a breeze upon the wind. And, like the Apostles who sat with Mary in stillness in the upper room waiting for the 'power from on High' that they had been promised by Jesus (the Holy Spirit He had breathed upon them and promised them a fresh outpouring of) – the Divine *ruach* that when it came arrived as tongues of flame and stormy winds that catapulted them into the streets to begin to wake the world anew to the 'good news' of the new creation that we are called to become – we will be called from our stillness to share the news of our soul, the image and likeness of God made visible in a world that is healed and renewed by the new creation with all of those who hunger to know who and what they are.

So then, if you would know your Soul anew, if you would step behind and beyond the brokenness of ego and the clinging attachment of desire to see the original beauty that God sees in you, then follow the path of breath and go inward into the inner chamber of the *nephesh*, to discover the living soul that you do not have, but that you ARE and then go deeper still and in that inner sanctuary in stillness await the discovery of the inbreathing of the *ruach* of God that already dwells there and know yourself to be a 'living Soul', created in the Divine image and likeness.

God created man in His image;
in the Divine Image He created Him;
male and female He created them.
Genesis 1: 27

The Lord God formed man out of the clay of the ground
and blew into his nostrils the breath of life,
and so man became a living Soul.
Genesis 2: 7

254

Prayer is a dialogue between life and life, between Divine life and human life, between the life of the spirit and the life of the flesh. Unless you enflesh the word of God, it cannot become real in the world.

I have asked the Lord for one thing;
One thing only do I want:
To live in the Lord's house all my life . . .

Psalm 27: 4

255

If you are willing to identify with other people
and try to understand them, some people may
see that as a weakness in you. But in fact, if
someone feels that you understand them and
that you see the validity of their point of view,
their attitude towards you can change and they
may view you in a more positive light. In this
way, countless complications and conflicts
can be avoided.

If we think about the vast majority of human problems,
both on a personal and on a worldwide scale,
it seems that they stem from an inability to feel sincerely
involved with others, and to put ourselves in their place.
Violence is inconceivable if everyone is genuinely
concerned with the happiness of others.

Matthieu Ricard

256

You may have picked up the idea over your lifetime that asking for help is a sign of weakness, and that makes it hard to look for help when you most need it. You may be afraid of rejection or of being laughed at for not knowing all the answers. But once you take the risk, make the leap and just ask, you are acknowledging that you can't do it all by yourself, you surrender to your own powerlessness, you give others the joy and satisfaction of helping you, and you can leave your fears behind in the past, where they belong.

He who is afraid of asking is ashamed of learning.

Danish proverb

257

When you pray you get in touch with reality, and reality gets in touch with you.

Prayer is the key of the morning and the bolt of the evening

Mahatma Gandhi

258

The practice of peace is the most vital and artistic of human actions. A peacemaker is like an artist who creates a painting, a dance, a symphony, a poem, respecting the contrast of light and dark, shadow and glare, tremor and quiet. It is the work of a lifetime, a work that promotes life.

If you wish to experience peace,
provide peace for another.

HH The Dalai Lama

259

The human desire for things to remain the same conflicts with the human desire for renewal, but the interplay of these two desires can bring you to strike a balance in your life.

Observe the life by cause and consequence.
Explore the life by wisdom.
Treat the life by equality.
Complete the life by love.

Buddha

260

It's your choice: you can give in to fearful preoccupations that shrivel your spirit or you can heed God's invitation to rejoice in who you truly are.

There is just one life for each of us: our own.

Euripides

261

It is certainly essential for you to grow into a more loving person, but it is equally important for you to accept yourself as you really are.

God is love, and he who abides in love abides in God and God abides in him.

1 John 4: 16

262

Imagine that your mind is like a shallow bowl filled with clear water. The bottom of the bowl is lined with pebbles and shells that represent all the things that clutter your mind – thoughts, feelings, tasks, commitments, the stuff of daily life. If you look through the water and see the busyness of your life slightly altered by the sheen of stillness, you can separate yourself from the doing, and instead just wait calmly.

Quiet is peace. Tranquillity. Quiet is turning down the volume knob on life. Silence is pushing the off button. Shutting it down. All of it.

Khaled Hosseini

263

Research has shown that people who are more
capable of identifying with others are also more
satisfied with their own lives.

If you want to go fast, go alone.
If you want to go far, go with others.

African proverb

264

Sometimes life is chaotic, and all you can do is say
yes and let yourself be led. At such a time, you
just have to trust that you will gradually be led
into a quiet place by what chaos theory calls the
'strange attractor' – this I believe, is God, the one
who leads you into a closer relationship of love.

One must still have chaos in oneself to be able
to give birth to a dancing star.

Friedrich Nietzsche

Breathing consciously is a well-known technique for centring yourself, calming yourself down, finding your way into a meditative state. It blocks out the voice of busyness and aerates the quiet corners of your mind.

The great thing about breathing consciously is that you can do it in public and nobody thinks you're weird. Breathing doesn't require accessories, special training or equipment – it's just breathing. You are doing it anyway; you might as well do it in a way that brings you peace.

Student, tell me, what is God?
He is the breath inside the breath.

Kabir

Don't allow yourself to become like a 'machine'.
Machines do not have relationships with families
and friends, machines do not raise children, laugh
or cry; machines do not feel joy as they watch the
sunset in amazement. Hang on to your humanity:
this is the reason you are in this world.

Joy is prayer, joy is strength, joy is love –
a net of love with which you can catch souls.

Mother Teresa

267

Peacemaking is not an optional extra in life. It is
your duty.

Peace I leave with you;
my peace I give to you.

John 14: 27

Most people like security, knowing where they are going and how they are going to get there. But society is in a constant state of transformation, and it is only in hope that you can navigate these changes.

The important thing to hang on to is the knowledge that when the unexpected happens, new possibilities open up before you. Like the seed that dies and brings forth new life, from brokenness and all kinds of troubles, disappointments and difficulties you can generate new inspiration, new questions, new ideas, new life, new hope and new solutions.

In a higher world it is otherwise,
but here below to live is to change,
and to be perfect is to change often.

John Henry Newman

269

As adults we tend to suppress our dreams, but it's
important to go on dreaming, to let the child in
you continue to dream the big dreams, because
you cannot accomplish what you cannot dream
or imagine.

If a little dreaming is dangerous,
the cure for it is not to dream less
but to dream more,
to dream all the time.

Marcel Proust

270

Every new day is a new opportunity to delight in life. Morning wakes not only your body but your spiritual being, opening you to all the gifts and graces that await you during this new day.

So, when you wake up in the morning, when the dawn breaks through the dark sky, allow it to rekindle your heart, and let the night open to reveal a new day. The sky is shining anew, and you too are part of that shining newness.

The breezes at dawn have secrets to tell you,
don't go back to sleep.

Rumi

271

If you think of everyone in your life to whom
you should be grateful, an interesting thing
happens. Bit by bit you realize that all you have
has come from other people: your parents and
teachers and the friends who have supported you,
helped you to feel good about yourself, colleagues
who have put you wise and taught you much of
what you know. Gradually you come to realize
that all you have – possessions, abilities, character
traits, ideals, values – comes from others or has
been evoked or inspired by the presence of
others.

*Do not forget the things your eyes have seen,
nor let them slip from your heart all the days of your life.*

Deuteronomy 4: 9

Every day, notice the small voice within that is trying to get through your fantasies of self-determination to send you messages.

If you look for the unexpected, and see your life in a spirit of openness, you will hear that small voice within and be surprised.

Everybody keeps telling me how surprised they are with what I've done. But I'm telling you honestly that it doesn't surprise me. I knew I could do it.

Ralph Waldo Emerson

273

When you are in great pain, you can't pray. It's just not possible. But in another sense, suffering itself becomes its own prayer. Suffering accepted becomes the mighty prayer to God. It was in pain that Christ redeemed you, and your pain continues that redemption.

I am the way, the truth, and the life.
No one comes to the
Father except through me.

John 14: 6

We live in a noisy world. Never before have people been so beset by distracting and disturbing sounds: whether it is traffic or machinery or music, planes flying over your head or the subways beneath your feet, you are subject to noise pollution all day, every day. These sounds enter your consciousness, vibrating in your mind, and little by little do invisible harm.

The only way to counteract this noisy invasion is to stop, consciously shut out distracting sounds, and listen, listen, listen – to what others have to say, and to what your own heart tells you.

To listen well is as powerful a means
of influence as to talk well, and is essential
to all true conversations.

Chinese proverb

If you live in right relationship with others, each loving act restores dignity, justice, liberation, reconciliation, forgiveness and peace.

Love the Lord your God with all your heart and with all your soul and with all your strength and with all your mind; and love your neighbour as yourself.

Luke 10: 27

276

Life lived from the centre of your being is a life of unhurried peace and power. It is simple, it is serene, it is amazing, and it is radiant. It takes no time, but it occupies all your time and it makes everything new and exciting. You need not fear: your Creator is at the helm, and when your day is done, you can lie down quietly in peace, and all is well.

Every day, think as you wake up, today I am fortunate to be alive; I have a precious human life, I am not going to waste it.

HH The Dalai Lama

I once read that when people in the West are asked about God, they tend to point to heaven, whereas people in the East tend to point to their chest.

I am certain both are right: the Divine God is above, below, behind, before and within us. The point of spiritual practice is to engage in dialogue with the Divine wherever you perceive it to be, whatever language you use about it, and however you have learned to speak to and listen to it.

God is always with you. Simply turn your face to him.

Kirpal Singh

278

The infinite beauty of God begins with the gift of life itself and continues with everything that sustains it.

*God gave us the gift of life, it is up to us
to give ourselves the gift of living well.*

Voltaire

279

Billions of people all over the world are suffering, are hungry, or are victims of injustice. It's impossible to ignore such huge difficulties, and yet it also seems impossible to do anything useful about them. These problems are so big that you probably can't imagine being able to do anything to help.

But what you can do is, in small ways, take a stand against injustice. And remember, the seemingly small things you do for others, the small acts of kindness, can have a major impact on their lives.

Be kind wherever possible.
It is always possible.

HH The Dalai Lama

280

It's easy to take the harmony of the world for granted: the sun rises; the moon follows its course, the tide ebbs and flows; the seasons change; and it all goes on happening, whether you notice it or not. But if you lose contact with the rhythms of nature, take them for granted, you can also lose your sense of the rhythm of your own life. That leads you to lose your sense of connectedness to the world, and you end by not seeing the universe as an interconnected system but as a collection of disparate parts.

If you choose, however, to live in harmony with yourself and with nature, you return to a vision of the world as one vast interacting pattern, and you come to recognize the part you play in that pattern, in the world.

How can you regard yourself as subject
and other beings as objects, when
you know that all are one?

Brihadaranyaka Upanishad

Pain can push you to the point of rebellion or despair. But it can also free you for creative transformation.

Whether suffering destroys you or becomes a source of creativity for you depends in part on you and your reaction to it. Nobody sets out to find suffering, but when it finds you, you can discern its value and gain from it.

*It is the crushed grape that gives out
the blood-red wine; it is the suffering soul
that breathes the sweetest melodies.*

Gail Hamilton

282

Humility gives you a desire for simplicity, and when you are simpler, you are also more genuine.

*Humility, that low sweet root,
from which all heavenly virtues shoot.*

Thomas More

283

The true benefits of generosity for the giver
are not material but an inner transformation.
When you give generously, you become more
open, more willing to risk. You set less store
on possessions and more on people, and the
barriers between you and others slacken,
so that you feel part of a whole in which it
is possible to share your resources, emotions
and yourself.

*The deepest principle in human
nature is the craving to be appreciated.*

William James

Sometimes it can be hard to let yourself be known, even by yourself. It's easier to hide from yourself.

It can help you to embark on your journey of self-knowledge if you realize that you are known completely and loved unconditionally by your Creator. You are known in the depth of your being, in the depth of yourself where you dare not look. You are known in the fullness and beauty that surpasses your greatest vision, dreams, hopes and imagination.

For you created my inmost being,
you knit me together in my mother's womb.
I praise you because I am fearfully
and wonderfully made.

Psalm 139: 13–14

285

Patience is a virtue that all good teachers have. They know how to wait for the student slowly to mature rather than pushing them before they are ready.

Patience is bitter but its fruit is sweet.

Jean-Jacques Rousseau

286

The cycle of life that gives way to newness does not happen without struggle. You are not usually asked, *Are you ready to change?* Change just happens.

Sometimes the process evolves so slowly that you hardly notice any movement: you simply wake up and find that you have come to another place. At other times, change happens in an instant, when you encounter the death of a loved one, the offer of a job, some pleasant surprise or perhaps a disappointment that you hadn't expected.

The rhythm of the seasons teaches you that continuity lies within the process of change and in the uprooting and replanting of your life. Hope not so much that things will turn out as you predict, as that you will be well amidst the changes you cannot predict.

*By feeling gratitude towards life,
I move towards light, wholeness, universal
energy, love. I move beyond the bounds of my
own life and discover that I am an expression
or form of universal life, or divine energy.*

Arnaud Desjardins

287

Discover what you love most, what your passion is, and then nurture and protect it and use it to help others. Life is God's gift to us, and what we make of that life is our gift to Him.

Our passions are the winds that propel our vessel.
Our reason is the pilot that steers her.
Without winds the vessel would not move
and without a pilot she would be lost.

Proverb

Friendship

John Quinn

I have always been intrigued by the story of the two disciples on the road to Emmaus in the wake of Jesus' resurrection. In Chapter 24 of St Luke's Gospel we are told they were 'conversing and debating about all the things that had occurred' as they travelled the seven-mile journey from Jerusalem to the village of Emmaus.

Apart from being told that they were disciples and that one was named Cleopas, we know nothing else about them – their means of livelihood, their business in going to Emmaus. I see them as close friends who are in particular need of each other at this dark time. Their Master has been crucified, and now comes the news that His tomb has been found empty. They are at once fearful and confused, but they find solace in voicing their opinions to each other. Why else would they be travelling together if not to support each other in their anxiety and loss?

A stranger draws near and walks with them. They are probably uneasy and suspicious at first, especially when his opening question is: 'What are you discussing as you walk along?' Cleopas, 'looking downcast', berates him. 'Are you the only visitor to Jerusalem who does not know of the things that have taken place?' And on being prodded further by the stranger, Cleopas pours out the story of the previous three days when they were hoping that the Nazarene 'would be the one to redeem Israel'. Now they are not sure what to believe.

The stranger suddenly changes tack and berates them. 'How foolish you are! How slow of heart to believe all that the prophets spoke!' And he proceeds to interpret the scriptures for them, with all those scriptures' references to Him. What an extraordinary journey this has become! Cleopas and his friend are beguiled by the stranger's insights and revelations. He has become a friend to them, so much so that they prevail on him to stop with them in Emmaus and have a meal. And it is only in the breaking of bread (significantly) that 'their eyes were opened and they recognized him'. In an instant he has vanished from their sight.

Far from being even more perplexed or frightened, the friends are ecstatic. Now they know. Now they are in the light. Now they are reassured. Then they said to each other, 'Were not our hearts burning within us while he spoke to us on the way and opened the scriptures to us?' They cannot wait to get back to Jerusalem and share their news with the other disciples.

The two friends had found a new common friend. One who knew when to listen and when to speak. One who spoke directly to their hearts which 'burned within them'. One who withdrew when their fears and anxieties were assuaged. Anyone who has a friend who makes the heart burn within is truly blessed. It is a singular feeling to experience that kind of friendship. It will banish sorrow, give balm to hurt, give strength to resolve. Being born out of love, it will seek no recompense but it will deserve gratitude. Cleopas and his friend were truly fortunate – they had found the One True Friend.

In the summer of 2001 I walked that road to Emmaus, metaphorically, when my wife Olive died suddenly while swimming in the sea. She had been part of my life for thirty-five years. It was a hard blow which left a raw gaping wound. In those first months after her death, I floundered in a sea of loss. I craved the steadying hand of friendship to help me stay afloat. I found it in the most unlikely of circumstances.

August 2001. I have resumed work as a radio producer in RTE. I take a bus into town to buy a book and decide to walk back to RTE. I break my journey in St Stephen's Green, mindful of the association of place with memory. Olive and I had sat here on a pleasant evening a year previously. People are enjoying a summer evening in the park. I light a cigar and try to relax with my memories.

Across from me, three homeless men lie sprawled on the grass. One of them rises and approaches me. 'Any chance of an ould cigar, boss?' (Why did I choose to stop in this place, now?) I offer him a cigar in the hope that he will leave me in peace with my memories. No doubt, I am 'looking downcast'. The homeless man sits down beside me and between cigar puffs proceeds, uninvited, to tell me his life story. Interpreting the scripture of his life, as it were.

His was a fascinating tale. He had been a successful jockey, married with children. On the instructions of an owner, he 'held' one or two horses (did not let them run a true race). He was summoned before the Turf Club, dismissed from racing and lost his licence. Everything went downhill from there. Unemployed, he turned to drink, became an alcoholic and eventually lost his home. His wife and children left him and he never saw them again. And now here he was, a homeless 'wino', cadging a smoke in a Dublin park. I thought to myself – there but for the grace of God go any of us. One or two wrong decisions and life is turned upside down.

He was a most articulate fellow, full of humorous asides and not objectionable in any way. In my own sorrow I enjoyed his company (did my heart burn within?). We finished our cigars and I stood up to go. For some reason I told him that I had lost my wife suddenly some six weeks previously. He stood opposite me, put his arms around me, leaned to my side and whispered in my ear, 'The seed in your heart will blossom.'

The poetry and brevity of his message stunned me. Confused, I turned to go. A few paces on I turned to wave him goodbye as he rejoined his mates. He mimed the message once again. I resumed my journey. A strange feeling had come over me. I felt an inner calm as I pondered over the strange words. There could only be one explanation. That was no 'wino'. That was Olive's messenger (and how typical of her sense of humour that she would send a smelly 'wino' and not a willowy blonde to deliver the message!). The message was one of reassurance and hope and it has stayed in my heart ever since. The seed (of love for Olive) continues to blossom wonderfully in my heart. The messenger vanished from my sight. Mission accomplished. I never saw him again but learned, sadly, a few years later, that he had been found dead from a drug overdose in a Dublin hostel. His name was Michael.

Michael had only been in my life for fifteen minutes

but it was a transformative event. He was the friend who offered his hand to calm me in that overwhelming sea of grief. His story lifted me out of myself. And his response to my one-sentence story was so poetic and perfect. I am thankful that I took the time to listen to Michael. I could easily have ignored him and walked off, but I chose to stay and will be forever grateful that I did.

Can a friendship be established in a mere fifteen minutes? Of course it can, especially when it touches the heart and makes it burn. That flame still burns within. I remember Michael every day of my life. He gave me hope. And faith. And love. I continue to draw on the 'deep waters (that are) the resources of the human heart' (Ecclesiastes 20).

Whether friendship lasts for fifteen minutes or fifteen years, its attributes remain constant. Adopting the model of Ecclesiastes 3, there is, regarding friendship:

> *A time to speak and a time to be silent;*
> *A time to act and a time to be still;*
> *A time to challenge and a time to console;*
> *A time to advance and a time to retreat;*
> *A time to admire and a time to admonish;*
> *A time to laugh and a time to weep;*
> *A time to praise and a time to pause;*
> *A time to listen and a time to leave.*

288

You may not ever take a seat at a negotiating table but at some time you will be challenged to be a peacemaker, where you are, in your parish, in your school or workplace, your family, your community.

Peace is a way of being that calls forth your deepest energies, requiring you to be constantly open to the new, to think with your heart, to strive continuously. It is a practice from which you can never withdraw.

A smile is the beginning of peace.

Mother Teresa

289

I knew somebody once who was unable to receive presents. Whenever anybody gave them something – a book, a box of sweets – they couldn't enjoy it. They were afraid of being in debt, and this stopped them not only from enjoying the book or the sweets but also from opening up to the other person.

To be grateful, you have to be without defences. You have to renounce your pride in order to recognize that your happiness depends on someone else.

Act as if what you do makes a difference.
It does.

William James

290

Let other people be who they are, for it is a good way in which to show respect. Do not limit them or surround them with judgements, advice, pressure or hopes about how they could or should be. You do well to trust that others can create their own destiny.

*Think for yourselves and
let others enjoy the privilege
to do so too.*

Voltaire

291

St Teresa of Avila tells us that there is a form of prayer called 'recollection', because the soul collects its faculties together and enters into itself to be with its God. Those who use this method can enclose themselves within this little heaven of the soul where the God of heaven and earth is present, and they can grow accustomed to being present there – free from distractions, where all too often our senses are drawn.

As thou art in church or cell that
same frame of mind carry out into the world
into its turmoil and its fitfulness.

Meister Eckhart

292

The way you approach your work is vital to your peace of mind, because it determines whether or not your work becomes love made visible or a burden to endure.

Pleasure in the job puts
perfection in the work.

Aristotle

293

Like everyone else, you are fragile. Sooner or later, you will be sick, make mistakes, fail or be disappointed in what life brings, and you will have to come to terms with your pain.

The best way to face pain is directly, with sincerity and courage. If you deny your suffering, it is hard for you to identify the pains of others. If you boast about it, you will see others as competitors and may not be sensitive to their problems.

Pain may dig deep, opening you violently and forcing you to discover emotions and resources you were not aware of. But it can also help you to develop your sensitivity, and connect you to others.

There is no education like adversity.

Benjamin Disraeli

If you want to act, you need to have a vision that drives your action. If you are faced with a task to do or a situation to resolve, you may tend to begin with action steps, but if you ask yourself why you are doing what you are doing, you can teach yourself to tap into the sacred space that lies within you, and out of which vision grows and gives meaning and purpose to your action.

Making peace is the same. You need to find in your heart a vision for peace that gives meaning and passion to your action for peace.

*Your sacred space is where you can
find yourself again and again.*

Joseph Campbell

295

You are called to move towards a future that is beyond you and beyond your control. This requires hope and trust in yourself and in those who are your companions on the journey, and hope and trust in the fidelity of God.

For the Lord is righteous, he loves justice;
upright men will see his face.

Psalm 11: 7

296

When you observe the Divine harmony in the world around you, how it permeates every aspect of life, the spiritual and the material, you can experience it with the eyes of your flesh and the eyes of your soul.

The beauty of a sunset, if you are watching it sensitively, is
shared by all human beings.

Krishnamurti

Surprise is the practice of accepting the unexpected interruption. And the practice of leaving enough space in the day for something to happen that isn't planned. Surrendering to surprise is the practice of balancing structure and order with openness. You may be surprised at the outcome!

Expect nothing.
Live frugally on surprise.

Alice Walker

298

Your most precious material things, even those you imagine will endure, are like sandcastles over which children squabble on the beach, and which are swept away at night when the tide comes in.

All human things hang on a slender thread:
the strongest fall with a sudden crash.

Ovid

299

Transformation depends on your capacity to be filled with the mystery of Christ. If you can make your being porous, then the mystery can enter you.

If you let yourself be ploughed, so that the furrows of your soul become deeper and deeper, and the earth of your being becomes softer and softer, then transformative grace can fill your heart.

> *Personal transformation can and does*
> *save the world. As we go, so goes the*
> *world, for the world is us.*

Marianne Williamson

300

Surprise encourages you to relate to experience with a sense of wonder. Surprise challenges you to be startled awake, shocked, perhaps, to the core.

Mystery is at the heart of creativity. That, and surprise.

Julia Cameron

301

Surprise is like opening a present. You can hardly resist shaking an unopened box to see what is inside, peeking under the corner of the wrapping.

But though life's surprises are sometimes delightful, they can also be painful. Life's surprises introduce unexpected elements and experiences you might not have had the courage to choose for yourself.

Our brightest blazes of gladness are
commonly kindled by unexpected sparks.

Samuel Johnson

302

Coming to believe that you are lovable is challenging but also healing.

You don't need to be accepted by others.
You need to accept yourself.

Thich Nhat Hanh

303

If you rush, you can lose yourself. But if you are too used to hurrying, you may not even notice the loss.

Tog bog e agus bogfaigh se chughat –
Take it easy and it will ease to you.

Old Irish saying

304

The great sense of relief that comes with gratitude comes from recognizing that you cannot manage alone, that you do not have to be a super-person, and that even if you are not so brilliant, you are fine as you are.

Gratitude is not only
the greatest of virtues, but
the parent of all others.

Cicero

305

Most people tend to live in their own heads, in their own little world, in their comfort zone, behind doors and windows that they do not open: front doors, office doors, car doors.

Open your door, and step out into the world. Go for a walk. Wander the streets, move outside your immediate neighbourhood, explore your town or area. Get connected with the world beyond your own little kingdom. Go out at a time of day when you don't normally do so. You never know what you might see or learn.

Taking a walk in a strange neighbourhood broadens your perspective and makes you a better, more aware and more connected citizen of the world. And of course it is also healthy and energy-giving. It invigorates your senses, your curiosity is engaged, your spirit starts to come to life.

He who neglects to drink
Of the spring of experience
Is apt to die of thirst
In the desert of ignorance.

Ling Po

306

Many liturgies include an invitation to offer a sign of peace to the people around you. In doing so, you are acknowledging that peace is within you. Perhaps you are prone to look for peace elsewhere. Maybe you find it hard to believe that you actually carry it within you. What would happen if you lived out of that peace you carry in your heart?

First keep peace within yourself,
then you can also bring peace to others.

Thomas à Kempis

307

Generosity loosens your grip on belongings and allows you to let go and be free.

Make all you can, save all you can, give all you can.

John Wesley

308

Fear may prevent you from being a person of courage and love. But if you allow the love that is deep within your being to take over your life, it will carry you forward, beyond fear.

With God on our side, who can be against us?

Romans 8: 31

309

Living in simplicity means living so that you rely on providence and appreciate the beauty of life. Simplicity fosters spontaneity, honesty and charity. Simplicity is necessary for anyone who seeks justice or peace, because it helps you to distinguish what is necessary from what is want.

I have just three things to teach: simplicity, patience, compassion. These three are your greatest treasures.

Lao-Tzu

310

To fight is to lose, and to lose is to be isolated and lonely. To surrender is to win, because when you surrender you are alive and connected with other people.

Surrender does not make you weak, it makes you humble; it forces you to admit to yourself and others that you are not perfect, you are human and make mistakes and that is fine.

Surrendering is faith that the power of love
can accomplish anything, even when you
cannot foresee the outcome.

Deepak Chopra

311

All humanity is one body, and you are a single cell. But each contributes to harmony and disharmony. If one little cell is malignant, cancer can spread and the whole body may be threatened. If one little cell is healthy, then well-being can also spread until the whole body is healthy.

You may never understand why you are the little cell that you are. You may never be able to see how your actions affect the larger whole. This is where faith comes in. Believe that you count.

In faith there is enough light for those who want to believe, and enough shadows to blind those who don't.

Blaise Pascal

312

There is a conformist and an outlaw in everyone.
Your challenge is to make room for that outlaw.
And also to make room for the conformist.

*Have a heart that never hardens, and a temper that never
tires, and a touch that never hurts.*

Charles Dickens

313

Gratitude is the basis of good health and well-being.
When you are grateful you will neither overestimate
nor underestimate yourself, because you are capable
of seeing the value in your actual situation. You
will appreciate what is good in your life.

*When all the work of the 'I' and the
'Mine' is dead, then the work of the Lord is done.*

Kabir

314

If you live always inside your comfort zone, according to your familiar daily routines, you can get stuck. Your opportunities to experience the excitement of each moment are reduced. Life is much more exciting if you choose to focus on the possibilities.

A dream is the bearer of a new possibility,
the enlarged horizon, the great hope.

Howard Thurman

315

Surrendering yourself to the possibility of something new and unknown will lead you to create something really important – a resilience to whatever life may offer you, good or bad.

We have more possibilities available in
each moment than we realize.

Thich Nhat Hanh

To be spiritual means to know and to live according to the knowledge that there is more to life than meets the eye. To be spiritual is to live knowing that God is present to you in grace as the principle of transformation. To be open to this is to accept who you are and who you are called to become.

Where there is charity and wisdom, there is neither fear nor ignorance. Where there is patience and humility, there is neither anger nor disturbance. Where there is inner peace and meditation there is neither anxiousness nor dissipation. Where there is mercy and discernment, there is neither excess nor hardness of heart.

St Francis of Assisi

317

There are people who by their nature are distressed at what might seem to you to be slight things. In these matters, do not judge by comparison with yourself; rather think of how you feel when you are at your weakest, and show compassion for this person's distress, regardless of the cause.

Be kind, for everyone you meet is fighting a harder battle.

Plato

318

A person who can miss all the green lights on the way to work and find a way to see it as a blessing is far better able to handle a problem at work, such as a misunderstanding or missed opportunities, and figure out the blessing in that event as well. It's all a question of having an attitude of gratitude.

Life is movement.
The more life there is, the more flexibility there is.
The more fluid you are, the more you are alive.

Arnaud Desjardins

319

Some years ago, Wangari Maathai saw her country, Kenya, torn by war and hunger and poverty. Its people were deprived of the basic necessities. Kenya, which was once green and lush and fertile, was disappearing. Wangari decided to start planting trees. It was a very simple idea but a very good one.

From Wangari's action of planting one tree at a time grew a national movement, and eventually thirty million trees were planted across Kenya.

You cannot live sheltered for ever without ever being exposed, and at the same time be a spiritual adventurer. Be audacious. Be crazy in your own way . . . Take risks, search and search again, search everywhere, in every way, do not let a single opportunity or chance that life offers pass you by, and do not be petty and mean, trying to drive a hard bargain.

Arnaud Desjardins

320

You do nothing alone. Life is lived in reciprocal
relationships: everyone is giving and receiving all
the time. Everyone is trading with everyone else,
even if you are not aware of it. Trust that the
contribution you are making is received and
passed around.

In nature, action and reaction are continuous.
Everything is connected to everything else. No one
part, nothing, is isolated. Everything is linked, and
interdependent. Everywhere everything is
connected to everything else.
Each question receives the correct answer.

Svami Prajnanpad

321

Gratitude exists only when there is solidarity and when all are agreed. Otherwise it is not gratitude at all, but a false or superficial optimism.

Let us be grateful to people who make us happy;
they are the charming gardeners
who make our souls blossom.

Marcel Proust

322

You have probably seen those optical illusions where, after you have gazed at a chaotic image, a coherent one emerges. It's the same with opportunities for generosity. All you have to do is look hard, and instead of seeing a boring routine you instead perceive occasions for being kind. You just have to pay a little more attention.

The present moment is filled with joy and happiness.
If you are attentive, you will see it.

Thich Nhat Hanh

323

Nearly everyone can find ways to stop themselves from enjoying life. Maybe you take yourself too seriously, or you only see what's going badly in your life.

It is surprising how just becoming aware of your own behaviour is enough to loosen the grip of self-destructive attitudes.

When the mind is full of memories and preoccupied by the future, it misses the freshness of the present moment. In this way, we fail to recognize the luminous simplicity of mind that is always present behind the veils of thought.

Matthieu Ricard

324

Everything that you say or do has the potential for good or evil, to create or to destroy. These two energies are very close. We all have some combination of these energies, and it is up to each of us, regardless of our way of life, to use these energies for creation or destruction. If your life is not about truth and goodness and beauty, then your creative energies are destroying not creating.

The worst enemy to creativity is self-doubt.

Sylvia Plath

325

Laughter gives you a new perspective on things. It is a great healer of spirits and hearts and it dissolves barriers between you and others. When you laugh with other human beings, you build bridges instead of walls. Laughter helps you to close the distances in your relationships. It is a true friend.

Even if you sometimes forget to invite it into your life, you can delight in welcoming it back.

If you are not allowed to laugh in Heaven,
I don't want to go there.

Martin Luther

Courage and Daring
and the Domesticity of a Spoon

Lelia Doolan

I came across a teaspoon the other day that I have had for years. It sits in the brown sugar bowl so it isn't used every day. It has a long history.

The stem is unusually long; it is slender and whorled. Its small deep bowl beams goldenly. There are filigreed markings of flowers and a heart on the back; maybe it is the mark of a coat of arms. It came from Russia with one of the families fleeing from St Petersburg after the assassination of Tsar Nikolai, his wife, their four children and their cook in July 1918. One of those flying families was called Truheart. They gathered up whatever they could in that frenzy and arrived in Finland. They were lucky enough to have a summer house in Karelia and they found shelter there.

Later on their youngest daughter, Nina Truheart,

married a Swedish-Finnish newspaperman. He was a steady and virtuous man. She was the tiny, voluble, shrewd and witty mother of a student friend of mine. On a holiday visit to that friend, I met her in Helsinki one summer. It was shortly after her beloved husband died and she talked about her sense of his loss. She put lighted candles around the house in the evening and liked to sit in their kind light as it brought him to mind. She talked about their flight when she was a young child and the memory of terror. As I was leaving, she gave me the spoon and the story of its journey. For me, it brought to life the tales of exile and endurance, of the violence of revolution, the displacement and death of countless millions of refugees then and since. The learned domesticity of exile. And how the aftermath of apparently revolutionary action forces other forms of courage on the bystanders.

The sorry fallout of ideas for change, and daring attempts to make new political arrangements can be a curse rather than a blessing. If only the powers would see their own corruption, their barren lust for power, and step aside for the new regime and become gardeners!

I don't know much about courage as an abstract idea. I've read about courageous people and heard about acts of daring and boldness. The way they tell it, such people seem to be outside the everyday run of things.

Mark Twain called Joan of Arc easily and by far the most extraordinary human being the world has ever produced.

Even though he was not a believer in her voices; 'I think they were saints, holy and pure and well meaning, but with the saint's natural incapacity for business. Whatever a saint is, he is not clever. There are acres of history to prove it . . . The voices meant Joan nothing but good, and I am sure they did the very best they could with their equipment; but I also feel sure that if they had let her alone her matters would sometimes have gone much better.' It is a wry comment on the absence of worldly wisdom among saints. Sounds quite true.

I saw a production of Shaw's *St Joan* in the Gate Theatre in Dublin long ago, with Siobhán McKenna playing Joan in a famous performance. It is the awesome story of a young, crisply direct, mystical country girl from Lorraine. In the fifteenth century she was convinced by voices, which she believed came from saints in heaven, that her destiny was to crown the dauphin, Charles VII, as King. He was a pretty lacklustre fellow who preferred a good treaty to a fight. She would have none of it. Her vocation was to unite all of France and free it from the English invaders. She became a soldier, wore men's clothes, led armies in victory as commander-in-chief, crowned the

King in Paris, was captured by Burgundians, sold on to the English, handed over by them to be put on trial by the pro-English Bishop of Beauvais, caged, threatened, frightened and finally burned at the stake as a heretic in 1431 in Rouen. She was nineteen years of age.

Twenty-five years later she was declared a martyr wrongly executed by corrupt partisan clergy abusing a Church trial for political purposes. In 1920 she was canonized. Behold familiar easy reparations. Too late, really, to be called courageous.

Courage for a cause is a dangerous business, and not just for the hero or the heroine. How heroic is a lot of what passes publicly for courage, in fact? Joan seems to have been a modest, innocent and vulnerable young person for one so daring, so steadfast to her cause, and so dangerous to others. Yes, Shaw has her say: 'I will dare, dare, and dare again in God's name', and when it is pointed out that she may find herself alone in the battle, she replies: 'I will not look back to see whether anyone is following me.' But he also quotes her reply during interrogation at her trial. She is asked if she is in God's grace. She answers: 'If I am not, may God put me there; and if I am, may God so keep me.' She was driven by an obsession. Her courage knew no fear until she was threatened by the real prospect of torture and the fire.

And of the soldiers who follow such heroes? They die in dreams of liberty and holy warring, in squalor and ignominy, led on by indentured role models with wills of granite. Whatever war is for, it has nothing to do with justice. It has nothing to do with courage, although it witnesses countless acts of self-sacrifice and human grandeur. Maybe Joan's saints had no grasp of that wisdom about war; maybe Joan's hearing was at fault. No matter which, she paid a terrible price. And thousands with her.

But so did Gandhi who refused that war. And Martin Luther King. And Jesus. And the brave millions who play out their own feats of heroism and daring and boldness and take risks every day of their lives. The man who jumped into a fast-moving river to rescue a pet rabbit; a teacher who stood in front of a demented gunman to save her pupils; one who stands up to the bully on another's behalf; any staunch inventor derided for innovation; a mother or father steadfast in their mundane tasks.

I remember all the faithful nobility of my own mother. It was not an obvious act of courage to face into every day with a true heart, into every sorrow and slight; to endure loneliness after our father's early death and all the anguish of that profound loss. This kind of courage all over the planet seems to me to come from a hard-won equilibrium, unshowy and benevolent. It is a kind of virtue.

And the daring and the risk-taking? It comes, I'd say, from doing the hard, repetitive, everyday thing without faltering. From finding a wild belief in the possibility of cheerfulness, of change, of a welcome for the possible. Seeking out a fresh solution. Making something new happen; some new life; some unexpected turn for the better. That's what people do out of their natural virtue. It has a long history; more tentative, more hidden than public gestures. Quite domestic, really; like the small teaspoon, equal to its daily role but faithful to a fabulous heritage.

326

You can seek the wisdom of God in prayer, but wisdom is also available to you through the ordinary events of your daily life.

He is not wise to me who is wise in words only,
but he who is wise in deeds.

Pope St Gregory I

327

The journey of life is a journey to find your true self, to find the garments that fit you. You have to stop pretending that you are somebody that you are not. Otherwise, you are wasting your life.

Where is there dignity without honesty?

Cicero

328

When my friend died, my emotions were mixed: love, appreciation, gratitude, grief, loneliness, emptiness, loss, sadness, frustration, anger and a whole lot more. What I learned from this experience was to live more deliberately and attentively, as he had lived, with integrity and attention. Life is short, but immensely valuable, and it is all too easy to move through life without experiencing it.

A humble knowledge of thyself is a surer way to
God than a deep search after learning.

Thomas à Kempis

329

If everything always went smoothly, people would take for granted all that is beautiful. We would not fully appreciate the gifts of life. We would be like spoiled children who have received so many presents they have grown bored. Indeed, sometimes it is the difficulties of life that open us to gratitude.

Struggle ends when
gratitude begins.

Neale Donald Walsch

330

You are a microcosm of the whole world, for we
all live in each other, and what you do counts,
however insignificant you may feel you are.

*Each of us is a unique strand in the intricate web of life, and
here to make a contribution.*

Deepak Chopra

331

In the face of the violence, destruction and
negativity of our world, you need a new kind of
courage: the courage simply to be the peaceful
and loving person that you are. If you achieve
this, then your actions will create security, your
words will create love and peace.

*You will never do anything in this world
without courage. It is the greatest quality
of the mind next to honour.*

Aristotle

332

It is difficult to accept that people you don't like and who may want to harm you are invited into the Kingdom of Heaven. The Gospel urges us to recognize in the stranger and the enemy the person of Christ.

Love your enemy, do good
to those that hate you, pray for
those who persecute you.

Luke 6: 27

333

All growth to fullness demands time. The seed must be buried before it germinates and grows. The earth must be ploughed and permitted to lie fallow or else it will wear out. In the autumn, nature becomes barren; winter waits for fertile springtime.

You too must face the winter of life, lie quiet and fallow for a while, because only in quiet and stillness can you hear the tiny whispers of life.

To the mind that is still,
the whole universe surrenders.

Lao-Tzu

334

In Genesis we read how God breathed into the dust of the earth in order to create us human beings. It is our job as human beings to keep these sources of dust and breath together. This is good work.

The goodness of God knows how to
use our own disordered wishes and actions,
often lovingly turning them to our advantage,
while always preserving the beauty of his order.

St Bernard of Clairvaux

335

True love is not possessive. It leaves you free to receive it or not, to respond to it or not. It is humble, willing to perform the humblest of tasks to meet the other's needs. It makes you sensitive to the other's gifts, needs and aspirations. It makes you compassionate and generous and self-sacrificing. It frees you to be yourself and others to be themselves.

In the evening of our life,
we shall be examined in love.

St John of the Cross

People who do not recognize their own value may tend to live superficially, so that they are less likely to be hurt.

People like this tend to change their mind easily; they tend not to be loyal. They are influenced by fashion and their relations are short-lived, possibly because they are opportunistic and self-seeking rather than loving and other-centred. It's not that people like this are bad; it's more that they are fragile.

Stronger people retain their integrity and for them it is natural to be faithful and trustworthy. They know how they feel, what they want and what they believe in. Their loyalty has roots in fertile ground and grows from clarity and inner strength.

There is no weapon more powerful in achieving the truth than acceptance of oneself.

Svami Prajnanpad

337

You cannot expect to find the full truth unless you continue each day to search and to ask what your time is saying to you, what it is calling you to do.

Have patience with everything unresolved in your heart and try to love the questions themselves.

Rainer Maria Rilke

338

Advent is a new beginning. It is actually a beginning and an ending. It ends an old life and begins a new life with Christ. You empty yourself so that the newness Christ brings can enter and have a place to stay.

I am the resurrection and the life . . .
Whoever believes in me will never die.

John 11: 25

339

The most sensible way to further your own
interest, to find your own freedom and to glimpse
your own happiness is to look after other people's
interest, help other people to be free from pain
and fear and contribute to their happiness. It is all
very simple: there is no choice between being
kind to others and being kind to yourself; it is the
same thing.

> *We are sometimes so occupied with*
> *being good angels that we neglect to be*
> *good men and women.*

St Francis de Sales

340

You have only this time now to live. You don't know about the next hour or hours or days. All that matters is that now you are present and you know it and you know why.

Write it on your heart that every
day is the best day in the year.

Ralph Waldo Emerson

341

The sense of belonging, the feeling that you are part of a whole greater than yourself is a necessary factor of human well-being.

If people grow up without truly being included by family and school or the community in which they live, they will feel there is something important lacking in their life; we all need to be important to other human beings, to have a place in this world where we are comfortable and secure. In seeking this sense of belonging, we can be led astray, joining groups that may be dangerous or threatening, like a gang or a cult; it can be hard to find a way out of this kind of situation. The typical profile of a young person at risk includes confusion of identity, alienation from family and friends, weak links with the community, feelings of impotence and an unfulfilled need for belonging.

Through the stairway of existence
We have come to God's Door.
We are People who need to love, because
Love is the soul's life.

Hafiz

342

The past, the present and the future are all one great universe. You have to trust that part of yourself that is most like God, that pure spirit within you and within the whole creation, that place of remembrance, which is the Divine within you, the Divine spirit which gathers us all into one.

To God, a thousand years are
like yesterday come and gone, no more
than the watch in the night.

Psalm 90

343

Listening is a way of showing respect, but it's a discipline you have to work at. Even if you really try to listen, you will probably find that all manner of thoughts and ideas and images flood your mind, and you find yourself waiting for the other person to stop talking and give you a chance to speak. You can't wait to have your say. Even if you don't actually interrupt, you have stopped listening.

True listening only happens in silence. You can only hear the other person when you have silenced the inner voices that distract you from what you are being told.

Listening itself is an art. When we listen with a still and concentrated mind, it's possible to actually be responsive to what the words are saying. Sometimes deep insights come in a flash, unexpectedly.

Joseph Goldstein

344

Reconciliation does not remove the injuries and wounds of the past. It is not a question of going back to the situation that existed prior to the oppression. What you must look for instead is something quite new, a state perhaps where the oppressor and the newly healed victim now become wounded healers who work separately or together to bring reconciliation to others.

A love of reconciliation is not weakness or cowardice.
It demands courage, nobility, generosity.
Overcoming oneself rather than one's adversary.

Pope Paul VI

The word *acedia* describes a nagging discouragement that can destroy your enthusiasm and self-esteem. It is a sluggishness that can rob you of your best self. It is a kind of negativity that can thwart your efforts to be joyful and committed. It can prevent you from seeing the great possibilities in yourself and others and takes away your ability to see the valuable contribution you can offer the world. It may even block all your positive response.

To combat *acedia* you need to challenge the negative voice in your head, and concentrate instead on the positive possibilities.

Nothing great was ever achieved
without enthusiasm.

Ralph Waldo Emerson

346

Simple acts of kindness give your life meaning. They heal and release in you and those around you the power to love and to spread love. They give courage and hope and empower others to reach out in love.

The best portion of a good man's life,
His little, nameless, unremembered acts
Of kindness and of love.

William Wordsworth

347

You come from God full of rightness, love and beauty and God is still at the centre of your being. You can go for many years with your beauty unknown and unaccepted by you. If you look and listen to your deepest self, you can grow to your full stature as God's work of art, a daughter or son of God. When you are fully human and truly yourself, it is God's glory that shines through you.

Beauty and the beautiful – these are one and the same to God.

St Thomas Aquinas

348

If a friend of yours suddenly becomes successful, what is your response? Are you happy for them, or do you feel a secret displeasure that the same has not happened to you? Do you make comparisons or wonder why you haven't been so lucky?

It is not easy to feel unconditional joy at the happiness given to someone else, but when you can, it means you have come a long way, and you know true joy.

*Only the intelligence of love and compassion
can solve all the problems of life.*

Krishnamurti

There are people who, on walking into a room, know how to assess the crowd, and within seconds can decide who is worth talking to, who is likely to be of use to them. This is a hard, harsh judgement.

To drop your judgements and accept people as they are when you meet them is a challenge, but it is a challenge that is worth the effort.

As you accept people openly and without judgement you will have the chance to truly connect with them, and these connections become tiny islands of trust. As your heart starts to change towards others, and theirs towards you, you will develop a sense of belonging to individuals, to various groups, to your community – you will find a home.

The golden way is to be friends with the world and to regard the whole human family as one.

Mahatma Gandhi

350

You are called to speak out, to name injustice and
to work to free and empower the oppressed.

*Our Good God asks of us very simple
and easy tasks: that our soul be united to God
by charity, that we do our duty as perfectly as
possible, that we do the most common
things in an uncommon manner.*

St Julie Billiart

Any new task, especially an important or difficult one, can cause anxiety. You can think of all sorts of reasons for not beginning a task. But the real reason is often a fear of failure. You don't want to look foolish or have people laugh at you or look down on you because you didn't do well or achieve what you set out to achieve.

The irony is that most people admire and respect someone who has tackled a major task, such as learning a new language, or returning to school after many years away – or perhaps it may be that someone has decided to take up a pastime that they have never attempted before. It is often acknowledged that trying new things takes a certain amount of courage and effort and we should never be afraid to try new things for fear of failing.

One who fears failure limits his activities.
Failure is only the opportunity to more
intelligently begin again.

Henry Ford

352

There is a reciprocity in giving. If you give, you receive. You cannot give without receiving; you cannot receive without giving. Giving and receiving is like a dance. If you don't ask for what you need, or you don't offer what you can, you block the dance. Imagine a person in the middle of the dance floor suddenly not moving while all around them continue; people start bumping into each other and losing the beat, losing their sense of direction. The dance is dependent on the dancer, and in the same way, the dance of reciprocity is dependent on unceasing exchange, of giving, receiving.

For it is in giving that we receive.

St Francis of Assisi

353

In the hidden parts of life, you can find forgotten or unsuspected treasures that you have not appreciated for want of time and attention. They are the gifts of life, some ordinary, some special. If you are distracted, you miss them. If you notice them, you are happier.

The invariable mark of wisdom is to
see the miraculous in the common.

Ralph Waldo Emerson

354

Others exist, each with their own needs, their realities, their hopes and dreams, their fears and their dramas, and you are one among millions of people on this planet, which is itself no more than a speck of dust in space. Your life is no more than a moment in vast universal time. Realizing and accepting this fact enables you to stay in your place and make room for others, and that in turn helps you to find your place in the world.

If you see the soul in every living being, you see truly.
If you see immortality in the heart of every
mortal being, you see truly.

Bhagavad Gita

355

To get the most out of life, you have to put effort into it, nurture and support your ideas and experiences. It is only when you're willing to try, to risk, to persist and to expend energy that you are rewarded by getting something out of what you're doing.

Allow your judgements their own silent, undisturbed development, which, like all progress, must come from deep within and cannot be forced or hastened. Everything is in gestation and then birth.

Rainer Maria Rilke

356

It is a good practice to reflect each night on the day that is drawing to a close. Look back on the people you have met, the situations you have been in, and ask yourself if you brought the good news to those around you. Ask yourself if people felt more complete or more beautiful or peaceful because of your presence. Then, in the morning, look ahead to the new day and consider who you will meet, and how you will greet them.

Reflecting and preparing in this way will help you to find God in the people you meet and will bring you joy and peace.

For this I bless you most:
you give much and know not that you give at all.

Khalil Gibran

357

Peace of mind is a spiritual state, waiting for you to find it. To experience peace of mind, you need to expand beyond psychological awareness and clarity and learn how to experience a wider range of awareness.

This is not as difficult or mysterious as it may sound; you have been doing it spontaneously all your life. A child climbs a tree, right up into the branches, and is held there by the wind and the sway of the tree, enthralled and enraptured, caught in the moment. The adult mind can also be held in the actual experience – wiped clear of explanation – and can exist in this moment in a pure state of relationship.

You may call this daydreaming or meditation, but whatever name you give it, this 'beyond world' experience is available to us all; we just need help remembering how to allow this awareness into our life.

The world is to the meditative man what the mulberry bush is to the silkworm.

Alexander Smith

358

Like everyone else, you have moments in your life when you are called to stand at the edge, where the possibilities before you are immense and the challenges mighty. These moments call for creativity, courage and hope.

At times such as this, put your hand in the hand of the Creator and move into the future, knowing that you will not be tried beyond your strength and the spirit who calls you will give you the gifts you need.

*Your belief determines your action
and your action determines your results,
but first you have to believe.*

Mark Victor Hansen

You were born in love and you are called to share that love.

What is your circle of love, how wide is it? Who is included, and who is excluded? Who is welcome, and who is unwelcome?

Take away love and our earth is a tomb.

Robert Browning

360

My mother always said, when God shuts a door,
He opens a window. She was reminding me to
look differently at surprise. It was an invitation to
trust the Divine as it works in our lives even when
the surprise is not to our liking.

What is more elevating and
transporting than the generosity
of heart which risks everything
on God's word?

John Henry Newman

361

True love has not to be earned, but is there for you, whether you respond to it or not. This is the love of a parent who loves their children so much that they desire nothing but the best for them and will go to endless trouble to meet their needs, to help them to realize their dreams; they love unconditionally and find happiness in the loving.

The ultimate lesson all of us have to learn is unconditional love, which includes not only others but ourselves as well.

Elisabeth Kübler-Ross

##

Winter brings cold, bleak days. Winter images of snow and bare trees, of ice and fog and murky afternoon twilight, invite you to embrace your own emptiness and befriend your darkness.

If you can empty yourself of yourself, you can make room for the One who will call you and tell you great and wonderful things.

> *Unless a grain of wheat falls to the ground and dies, it remains only a single seed. But if it dies, it produces many seeds.*

John 12: 24

363

Humility helps you to shake off your fantasies and touch reality as it is. It helps you to see that you are one among many, mortal and limited. You are a human being amongst other human beings, and you don't have to prove yourself to anyone.

True humility makes no pretence of being humble, and scarcely ever utters words of humility.

St Francis de Sales

364

If you can bring relief and well-being to just one other person's life, this is a victory worth having: a silent, humble response to the suffering and pain on this planet. Your small kindnesses are not only capable of saving humanity, they are already saving it.

At the touch of love, everyone becomes a poet.

Plato

365

Life unfolds in mystery, and your journey into mystery is guided by the inner light of faith, which shines from the core of your being, where dwells the Divine, whether you are aware of it or not.

For me to live is Christ, and to die is gain.

Philippians 1: 21

Belonging

Sister Stan

The need to belong is probably the least-recognized need of the human heart. Our need to feel connected is dense and desperate, and if we do not feel that we belong – to a place, to a person, to a community – we are rootless, abandoned and miserable.

To belong is to be part of a community – a family, a network of friends or colleagues, a neighbourhood, a class, a club, a team, a society, a union or professional organization, a band or choir or drama group, a political party or a social campaign. It is not enough to be a member of such a group: to feel that we belong, we need to feel that our participation in the group is valued, and that the group cares about us not just as group members but as individuals.

Our home is a physical expression of our belonging to a family and a neighbourhood. The first thing we ask

when we meet a new person is *Where are you from?*
Where do you live? Where is your home? And we
answer by naming our city or village, our street or
neighbourhood. I live here, we are saying, this is my
locality, my place, I belong here, the people around me
are my family, my neighbours, and some of them are my
friends. As Brendan Kennelly puts it in his poem, 'We
are living':

> *What is this room*
> *But the moments we have lived in it?*
> *When all due has been paid*
> *To gods of wood and stone*
> *And recognition has been made*
> *Of those who'll breathe here when we are gone*
> *Does it not take its worth from us*
> *Who made it because we were here?*

And Vona Groarke likewise writes, in 'Home', about how
the physical place we call home is imbued with our
emotional attachment to the sense of safety and belonging
that it gives us:

> *I always thought this house would keep us safe*
> *as when running from the car to the front door late at night*
> *I knew it was where darkness could not reach.*

In her famous book about living on a tiny island off the coast of Kerry in the early part of the last century, Peig Sayers wrote *Ar scath a chéile a mhaireann na daoine* – the people live in each other's shadow. In her small island community, the people survived by co-operating with each other, by living in community. Humans need to co-operate for practical reasons but also, and crucially, in order to feel connected, to belong, to be able to reach out and almost touch the bonds that tie them to each other and to their locality. Because it is that sense of belonging and connectedness that keeps us rooted, keeps us sane, gives us a sense of contentment. If we lose that sense of connectedness and belonging we lose our sense of self and ultimately we lose our sanity and our ability to cope, and when we do we are on a downward spiral to unhappiness.

When a person loses their home, they lose much more than an address and a place of comfort and safety; they lose their sense of belonging to a place, to a family and to a community. Since they no longer belong, the homeless person feels uncared for. Does anybody care that I have no place to go tonight? Does anyone care that I am hungry or thirsty, does anyone care that I am cold and wet, does anyone care that I am sick? Does anybody care if I die tonight? The homeless person knows that the answer to all these questions is No, because they no longer belong, and that is the greatest hardship of the homeless: not the cold or wet or violence of street culture, but the feeling of belonging nowhere, with no one to care about their needs.

What the homeless person has lost, above and beyond their physical home, is their sense of belonging and their sense of community. Community is precious and we know it, but it is not a self-sustaining thing. It does not keep on recreating or reinventing itself. It doesn't just happen – it needs to be built and nurtured by neighbour greeting neighbour, by different ways of involvement in the community and all the mutualities that knit strangers over time into a caring, functioning community. Today technology has a lot to offer to keep us connected but it is also true that in a society where electronic communication is so easy we are in danger of losing the personal touch. People often don't know their neighbours. It is in reaching out to others with a welcoming handshake, a listening ear, a pat on the back, a shared tear, that we reveal our humanity. This is what brings us close and gives us a sense of belonging as well as building community.

Belonging is not all about feeling cared for by our community. Not only do we need to know that we have allies, especially in time of trouble, but we need also to feel that we are allies to other people and that they depend on us as well as us depending on them. It is in others' company that we flourish, as each one of us puts our unique talents at the service of others. When we feel we belong, we are in a strong position to make others also feel part of that belonging.

The need to belong is spiritual as well as emotional. We also have a longing to belong to God. In the deepest part of our being, at that still point, there is a longing and a yearning for something beyond the material, whether we recognize it or not. St Augustine recognized it when he said, 'Thou has made me for thyself, O Lord, and my heart will never rest until it rests in thee.' Jesus recognized it too when he said, 'Make your home in me as I make my home in you, abide in my love.'

And Jessica Powers describes the sense of spiritual homelessness in her poem:

> It is the homelessness of the soul in the body sown;
> it is the loneliness of mystery:
> of seeing oneself a leaf, inexplicable and unknown,
> cast from an unimaginable tree;
> of knowing one's life to be a brief wind blown
> down a fissure of time in the rock of eternity.
> The artist weeps to wrench this grief from stone;
> he pushes his hands through the tangled vines of music,
> but he cannot set it free.

This December Day

Brendan Kennelly

Here in this room, this December day,
Listening to the year die on the warfields
And in the voices of children
Who laugh in the indecisive light
At the throes that but rehearse their own
I take the mystery of giving in my hands
And pass it on to you.

I give thanks
To the giver of images,
The reticent God who goes about his work
Determined to hold on to nothing.
Embarrassed at the prospect of possession
He distributes leaves to the wind
And lets them pitch and leap like boys capering
*   out of their skin.*

Pictures are thrown behind hedges,
Poems skitter backwards over cliffs,
There is a loaf of bread on Derek's threshold
And we will never know who put it there.

For such things
And bearing in mind
The midnight hurt, the shot bride,
The famine in the heart,
The demented soldier, the terrified cities
Rising out of their own rubble,

I give thanks.

I listen to the sound of doors
Opening and closing in the street.
They are like the heartbeats of this creator
Who gives everything away.

I do not understand
Such constant evacuation of the heart,
Such striving towards emptiness,

Thinking, however, of the intrepid skeleton,
The feared definition,
I grasp a little of the giving
And hold it close as my own flesh.

It is this little
That I give to you.
And now I want to walk out and witness
The shadow of some ungraspable sweetness
Passing over the measureless squalor of man
Like a child's hand over my own face
Or the exodus of swallows across the land

And I know it does not matter
That I do not understand.

Contributors

to *Day by Day*

Tony Bates
Dr Tony Bates is a psychologist and the Founding Director of Headstrong – the National Centre for Youth Mental Health, in Ireland. He is an *Irish Times* columnist and author of several bestselling books on depression including *ComingThrough Depression: A Mindful Approach to Recovery*.

Lelia Doolan
Lelia Doolan has worked in theatre, television, film and journalism, has done a bit of teaching, is active in cultural and environmental issues and is currently involved in building an arthouse cinema in Galway.

Anna Fiona Keogh
Anna Fiona Keogh is a dance movement psychotherapist

based in Dublin, where she facilitates creative movement and dance workshops and also has a private practice.

Mark Patrick Hederman
Mark Patrick Hederman is abbot of Glenstal Abbey, a Benedictine monastery in Limerick, where he has been a monk for over forty years. Formerly headmaster of the school, he has lectured in philosophy and literature in many countries, as well as in Ireland. He is a founding editor of the cultural journal *The Crane Bag*, and author of several books, including *Kissing in the Dark*, *Underground Cathedrals* and *Dancing with Dinosaurs*. His most recent book is *The Boy in the Bubble: Education as Personal Relationship*, published in 2012.

Brother Richard Hendrick
Brother Richard is a priest-friar of the Irish province of the Capuchin Franciscan order. For the past twenty years he has worked to bring the riches of the Christian contemplative tradition to young people at both second and third levels. He is one of the founders of the 'Sanctuary for Schools' programmes developed at the Sanctuary, Stanhope Street, Dublin, which seeks to offer the wisdom of the different world meditative traditions as an answer to the challenges many young people face on the path to adulthood today.

Currently, Brother Richard resides in Cork where he is the head of Chaplaincy in University College Cork.

John Quinn

John Quinn is a former teacher and award-winning radio broadcaster. He retired from RTE Radio in 2002 after a 27-year career there. He has written six children's novels, one adult novel, two memoirs and a number of books related to his radio career. His most recent book is *Moments*, published by Veritas in 2011. He lives in Co. Galway.

Sister Stan

Sister Stanislaus Kennedy joined the Irish Sisters of Charity in 1958 and has become one of the most influential social innovators of her time. She has received awards from many universities and institutions in Ireland and elsewhere, and founded Focus Ireland, the Immigrant Council of Ireland and Young Social Innovators. She also established The Sanctuary, a place of peace and meditation set in the heart of Dublin. Sister Stan has written several bestselling books, including her autobiography, *The Road Home*, *Seasons of Hope* and *To Live from the Heart*. Her international bestseller, *Gardening the Soul*, has recently been reissued. She lives in Dublin.

Síle Wall

Síle Wall is a Religious Sister of Charity and has worked for many years as a social worker with people on the margins of society especially on issues related to mental health, learning disability and homelessness. She has been involved in the development of the Sanctuary since it was founded in 1998 and currently practises there as an art therapist as well as facilitating meditation/mindfulness practices and workshops.